SUC[ ]
COMPANY

George Forbes

Lang**Syne**
PUBLISHING
WRITING *to* REMEMBER

About the author

George Forbes was born in the Glasgow shipyard district of Linthouse in 1948. Leaving Govan High School in 1965, he became a reporter with the *Scottish Daily Express*. He has also worked on the staff of the *Daily Record*, *Scottish Daily News* and *the Herald*. In his years in journalism he covered countless crime stories in Glasgow and thanks to investigations into the Paddy Meehan case was one of those instrumental in getting that injustice put right (Meehan subsequently helped with the research for this book). Married and living on the outskirts of Glasgow, Mr Forbes is currently Consultant Editor of the popular monthly history/nostalgia magazine *Scottish Memories*.

Lang**Syne**

PUBLISHING

WRITING *to* REMEMBER

Vineyard Business Centre,
Pathhead, Midlothian EH37 5XP
Tel: 01875 321 203 Fax: 01875 321 233
E-mail: info@lang-syne.co.uk
www.langsyneshop.co.uk

Design and artwork by Roy Boyd
Printed by Blissetts
© Lang Syne Publishers Ltd 2004
Reprinted 2008 and 2010

ISBN 978-1-85217-019-6

SUCH BAD COMPANY

contents

Illustration: Artist's impression of Bible John

INTRODUCTION

This is a fascinating catalogue of crime in Glasgow's underworld during what might be described as its black heydays, that is before drugs were introduced, before murder became squalid and commonplace and at a time when not only the crimes themselves held individual aspects of interest but also the criminals were 'characters'.

The original research for this book was undertaken with the late Paddy Meehan, safecracker and Gorbals criminal, with whose help I was able to talk to the dying breed of the old-style Glasgow hard men and bad boys.

The resulting book, *Such Bad Company*, was first published in 1982 and became over the years something of an underground cult classic as it gradually went out of print. The number of inquiries I have had as to where it might be purchased over the years are now legion and I'm glad to say that here the most interesting chapters have been reprinted.

Some things, of course, have changed over the years. Paddy Meehan himself died of throat cancer in 1994 and Ian Waddell, the killer who committed the crime of which Meehan was wrongly convicted, ended up strangled and buried in a Glasgow tenement's back court after a drunken argument with another criminal. Jimmy Boyle was eventually released after having served 15 years and went into business in Edinburgh as a wine importer. He helped in voluntary work with junkies but a son he had from a teenage relationship was stabbed to death near the Gorbals over a dispute about drugs. Meanwhile, the Scottish Office closed the Special Unit in 1994, claiming it had outlived its usefulness.

But otherwise this celebrated saga about the bloody, dark secrets of the city is as valid and intriguing as when first published. Here are recounted the exploits of serial killer Peter Manuel, the psychopath who terrorised the populace till his craving for publicity trapped him; Gentle Johnny Ramensky, the Great Escaper; the Razor Gangs of the 1930s; cop killer Howard Wilson; Walter Scott Ellis who cheated the gallows; the Meehan case, full of intrigue and sinister espionage; Jim Griffiths who turned the streets into a caricature of prohibition Chicago; Jimmy Boyle, the gangster who came good; as well as a cast of many minor crooks.

My view has not changed that crime just is not what it was. In the pre-Thatcher world depicted in this book there was, more or less, full employment and violence was a rarity. Drugs were a minor, fringe nuisance, not a major plague. When I became a reporter in the mid 1960s, murder was always a front page story and each one usually had its unique aspect, unlike nowadays where it is so commonplace that such crimes often hardly rate a mention,

I would remind readers that certain statistical references and comments pertain to conditions in 1982 rather than 2004 and would also point out that for this edition the running order of chapters has been altered.

Many are the tales that could be told of crime in Glasgow but this is a selection of what might be termed the best cases and I hope you find them enthralling and exciting.

George Forbes, July 2004

Chapter one:
CHILDREN OF THE NIGHT

Glasgow is synonymous with gangs just as it is with slums and the first were created by the second. The tradition of the organised gang or team of teenagers or young men, territorially organised into groups who wage war with weapons such as knives, razors and hatchets purely for the violence and the glory, is a phenomenon unusually characteristic of the city and not found in such abundance or historical length anywhere else in Britain.

There are other grim factors unique about the city. According to Alcoholics Anonymous the drink problem is three times as high as anywhere else in Britain, Glasgow being the alcoholic capital of western Europe. Hard boozing has been characteristic of the place for a hundred years. It also has the worst housing in Europe with more overcrowding, more sub-standard and more municipal dwellings than any other comparable city, allied to a 'brain drain' of talent away from areas euphemistically labelled in typical modern jargon as suffering from "multiple urban deprivation" meaning verminous slums riddled with crime and despair. And again this has always been the case since the Industrial Revolution.

During periods of recurrent recession Glasgow has always had the unenviable position of being among the leaders in the unemployment league and recently with the decline of major industries such as shipbuilding and heavy engineering the unemployment rate has been running well ahead of most of the country yet again. It is something the city should be used to by now since there was one in three adult males unemployed in the thirties at a time when Glasgow boasted it was the second biggest city in the British Empire. It also has suffered a high general early death rate and the worst rate of lung cancer and heart disease in Britain, as well as, up until recent years, one of the worst rates of rickets and similar children associated diseases.

It has also been one of the most violent areas in Britain ever since it was designated a city and it has a prison population far above the European average.

With all of these grim records concentrated in the valley of the Clyde, it is hardly surprising that other bizarre manifestations have sprung up, among them gangs.

The Celtic temperament common to both Scots and Irish has several broad tendencies: a natural aggression (possibly spawned from an inferiority complex), sentimentality, a belief in man as the hunter and woman as the housewife-cum-mother and a propensity for high spirits in the shape of whisky or whiskey or *us'quebaugh* as the Gaels called it, meaning 'Water of Life'. They also have a centuries old obsession with religion whether Roman Catholic or Presbyterian. Just as it was Cromwell's transplanting of dour, aggressive Protestant Scots to Northern Ireland which sowed the seeds of Ulster violence, so the influx of Irish Catholics and Orangemen into Clydeside shipyards led to another of Glasgow's unenviable peculiarities, the Rangers - Celtic syndrome.

The Irish Catholic immigrant workers brought over during the Industrial Revolution and the native Protestant Scots of similar religions picked out two rival football teams, for the Protestants the blue shirted Rangers south of the city and for the Catholics the green shirted Celtic in the East End, to symbolise their religious differences on the sporting field and transpose their vigorous theological hatreds from the churches and the chapels to the terracings. Celtic was originally started as a club to provide soup kitchens for the poverty stricken Irish and the early feeling against them was a resentment at the encroachment of these job hungry settlers. But later the anti-Catholic element replaced the ethnic one.

Rangers were formed by Protestant shipyard workers brought over from Ulster to start up a subsidiary of Harland and Woolf's on Clydeside and the bigoted polarisation and rivalry of these two teams supporters became a logical if deplorable extension of their religious differences which regularly erupted into violence.

Every time this century the teams have met in sporting combat the fans, with their banners and war cries, have joined in off-the-field fisticuffs, bottle throwing and general mayhem. This on a grand scale where Chief Constables are still regularly quoted as saying crowds are well behaved when there have been only 200 arrests. It is the same as what happened on a smaller scale in gangland, although in both cases religion, like territory, was and is not so much a reason in itself as an excuse for identifying and belonging to one group to take out animal frustration on another.

The seeds then were there for gangs from the beginning: overcrowded slums, poverty and ignorance, a need to assert oneself, a sudden large influx to the working class which nevertheless was frequently unemployed, and a pronounced tendency for drink also viewed as a test of manliness, all of this peppered with a good dose of religious bigotry.

The first organised groups of brawlers sprang up in the 1880s at street corners and pubs among the city's sprawling tenements in the East End. They started a tradition, followed by their future blood brothers over the years whereby a common fund was set up to pay fines and hence the first Glasgow gang got its name - 'The Penny Mob'. At this time there were frequent encounters with the police and court reports gave the leaders of the packs the rather stuffy title of 'chairmen'.

The Penny Mob bred rivals such as the San Toy Boys from Calton nearer the city centre and the Tim Malloys, the Calton mob's war cry as they charged into street battles being "We are the young San Toys and we can fight the Tim Malloys!"

The South Side, later to become a notorious breeding ground for the worst or best gangs depending on your viewpoint, came up with the Mealy Boys, the McGlynn Push and the picturesquely-named Gold Dust Gang, although the Gorbals never produced a prospector.

The average age of the gang member was twenty and in some areas it was not only a test of manhood but also advisable for the health to have the support of your local lads when inky nights were dimly punctured by gaslight and eyes could be watching in the dark.

Frequently the drinking dens where the gangs held out and boosted their courage were raided and wrecked by rivals. And passers-by were by no means immune from blows.

Sporadic mayhem continued into this century and even the drain of young men into the mass muddy graves of the First World War seems to have had little effect on gangland manpower. There always seemed to be someone young and eager to fill a hooligan's shoes until he too was marched to the front. There were more than a million inhabitants of the city by 1914 which provided plenty of cannon fodder for strife at home and abroad.

The Redskins took over the East End as their happy hunting ground and fought such worthies as the Calton Black Hand, the Bloodhound Flying Corps, the Hi-Hi's and the Hazel Bells from Mile-End and Bridgeton, the Kelly Boys from Govan and the Baltic Fleet from Baltic Street. The Redskins claimed they 'ruled' their area, the first time the expression was used, and also boasted an organised membership of a thousand who had a loud, quick, tuneless whistle whereby a member could gather fast support to his side should rivals set about him, always assuming he could get the whistle off in time and that a courageous pal was in the neighbourhood to hear it and not run the other way. The Redskins also disdained fists as kids stuff, much preferring a swashbuckling meat cleaver or hammer. They also moved into crime by getting protection money from shopkeepers and tradesmen who were scared they would get their premises wrecked. Pedestrians were attacked and robbed openly in daylight in the street. The police eventually decided the Redskins should be tamed. They clamped down heavily, made raids and arrests, and cajoled witnesses into speaking and reasserted their particular rule. Among weapons uncovered under beds, in wardrobes and below floorboards were knives, heavily leaded batons of wood and rubber, revolvers, iron bludgeons and steel clubs. A myth has grown up that the old gangs fought only among themselves and while this was generally true it was by no means always the case.

Instead of 'chairmen' gangs now had their 'Kings', an indication of the growth of the pastime. They also had their 'Queens', the wildest and usually most good looking girls in that particular block of slumland. It was quite an honour to hold court and girls were eligible as soon as puberty was reached. The age of consent was not a nicety which bothered the gangs and in true Hollywood tradition, although the cinema had not yet arrived to show them, the molls were as hard talking, brassy and 'gallus', or sharp, as their counterparts while holding their liquor and opening their legs on order. Some of the girls even took part in the fights, probably to prove they were not girls at all, but invariably they ended up at the Royal Infirmary. These girls normally dropped out before their twenty-first birthdays when the inevitable baby came along. They took their place as house-keeper in the male dominated society, taking up the traditional chores of changing the nappies or frying the sausages, or taking the laundry to the 'steamie' and could be seen leaning, like haggard, aproned figureheads with curlers and fags from their windows chatting to neighbours and watching the world go by.

With the end of the Great War (during which shipyard production had reached its all-time peak) and the coming of the twenties, the spectre of unemployment, which always hovered round the corner in Glasgow, crept back to haunt the slum dwellers. The average age group of the gang leaders gradually became older as discontented cloth-capped young men lounging 'on the burroo' at street corners decided to revolt in their own way just like their teenage counterparts. Now with more muscle, more cunning and more bravado amongst the bulky, brawling hooligans, gang battles became more organised, bigger in numbers and more deadly.

Throughout the twenties and thirties there were regular pitched battles between rival gangs from north and south sides involving hundreds of screaming, weapon wielding hooligans. There were also more sedate 'fair fights' or 'square goes' between stripped-to-the-waist gang leaders on Glasgow Green without any Queensberry rules, just brute fist and foot smashing where they could, but even these generally degenerated into a free-for-all. Sometimes the police were quite content to stand by and let them knock hell out of each other and then step in and pick up the pieces in the hope that the arrogance would be crushed out of the damaged remains after a spell in hospital and prison. Sometimes this led to the breaking of a gang leader but it also led to others escaping and enhancing their reputation.

The Gorbals, that sprawling district on the south bank of the Clyde, bred the best fighting stock. It also pioneered the use of a new weapon, the open razor, and invented a new phrase 'razor slashing', a particularly ghastly and arbitrary way to slice up a victim. Among other favourite weapons were Ghurka knives, bayonets, pokers and broken bottles.

Favourite haunts included the many dance halls dotted throughout the city at this time. The gang members would 'jake up' on potent fortified red wine which they could buy for 3d a gill and show off their girls at 'the jiggin''. Frequently there were fights between the girls over a particularly virile gang member, hair tearing, face scratching, screaming scraps, casually and laughingly watched by jibing, onlooking males.

Like most Glasgow gangs, serious crime was a peripheral and not an integral part of their activities. Their raison d'etre was simply to bash other people's heads in, cut them and hold onto their district in a primitive machismo-like style which fed stultified egos with a feeling of importance. The more adult and organised the gang the more crime there was, the traditional ones associated with such groups, like extortion and theft. They also organised local shebeens, illegal drinking dens, often just a room and kitchen with a drink laden table where the thirsty could get a drink outside the prohibitive licensing hours if they were willing to pay hefty prices for stolen liquor. Illegal moneylending with extortionate interest rates also became a feature of the more organised gangs of the sixties and this worked hand in pint with the shebeens.

It was a good breeding ground for the lifelong criminals. A man who was handy with his fists when young could be lucratively employed by bigger fish when he was older. But although many of the active members ended their short careers rotting in prison, their bodies prematurely aged through abuse, there were equally many others who lapsed out of their wilder than wild oat days and succumbed to a miserable domesticity and respectability rather than a life of crime. And if they had been lucky enough to escape 'the jailers' they could bring up their children safe in the knowledge that they had no record and in fact had committed no crimes except bash about others as violent as themselves.

In a sub-cultural manner it was the same as junior football teams playing each other, except instead of a ball and boots being used to let out youthful animal spirits it was knives and coshes being utilised to ventilate their hatreds. Perhaps this is why gangs gradually changed over the years to calling themselves teams because the former has overtones of big time syndicates while the latter has a more suitable feeling of young recklessness. Although tales of gang warfare became exaggerated by the pint swilling exuberant victors, their exploits rarely rose above an armed clash in the street, sometimes organised, sometimes accidental.

In the thirties the Bee Hive gang were the Kingpins in the Gorbals but it was a near run thing holding their ground against such battalions as the Billy Boys, Stickit Boys and Derry Boys from Bridgeton, the Antique Mob from Shettleston, the Black Diamond Boys, the Hammer Boys and the Dirty Dozen from the South Side, the Romeo Boys from the East End and the Kelly-bow from Govan.

The Bee Hive's territory was the Cumberland Street area of the Gorbals. It's leader was a man named Peter Williamson who, because of his prowess as a fist fighter, became a legend in his own day.

The Bee Hive was a bigger threat to the citizenry than most gangs of that era because its members concentrated on money making ventures like shop-breaking and safe-blowing. This did not mean that they were averse to doing battle with any other Glasgow gang. When the necessity arose to settle differences with some other gang then Peter Williamson would send a message to the leader of the gang involved, inviting him to single combat. If the other leader accepted the challenge then he and Peter, accompanied by their seconds, would meet at some secluded spot on Glasgow Green. There they would fight it out, and afterwards shake hands and go off to the nearest pub or shebeen for a restorative drink.

With the outbreak of the Second World War, the Bee Hive gang broke up. Petter Williamson went off to the army where he was soon promoted to the rank of sergeant. After the war Peter went back to safe blowing for which he was to serve a couple of sentences at Peterhead Prison.

Around 1930 religious bigotry spread its fiery torch through the city with the rise in the East End of the Billy Boys who were rabid Orangemen (they took their name from 'King Billy', the Prince of Orange). Their arch Catholic enemies were the Norman Conquerors (known better as the Norman Conks) whose H.Q. was in Norman Street.

In 1935 on all Catholic Saints and Holy Days the Billy Boys Drum and Flute Band, led off by their prancing, pirouetting, 'pipe major' leader Billy Fullerton, would march down Norman Street playing rousing Orange tunes. Each time this happened the Conks let fly from their windows and roofs a hail of bottles, bricks, pickshafts and buckets of excreta down on the immaculately sashed musicians who would continue to make their haphazard, out-of-tune way to church where, instead of going in, they would simply disband. So much for religious feelings. The chaotic marches were finally and truly disbanded and the flutes silenced by a full-scale charge of mounted police who scattered the Orangemen and dealt baton blows from their horses to the nearest Billy Boys. One of the gang, Elijah Cooper the big drum player, escaped injury by diving into his instrument and, using it as a shield, rolling away from the thundering hooves of the police.

The Billy Boys had kept up the tradition of the Penny Mob because each of the eight hundred men commanded by Fullerton carried membership cards on which a weekly 2d payment had to be marked up. At one stage there was more than £1,200 in their local bank lodged under three names and it was used for fines and keeping wives whose breadwinners had been jailed. Some local shopkeepers were also 'asked' to contribute. It was Fullerton's brainwave to lift £600 to form the flute band as a way of emphasising their contempt of the Conks.

No Billy Boys wedding was complete without a certain robustness. On one occasion, fearing a Conks intervention while one of the Billy's lieutenants was getting married, Fullerton arranged for the bridegroom to be at the altar with a sword concealed in his morning dress, the best man with a gun in his pocket, a guard of honour holding razors instead of swords and finally, seeing there was to be no battle after all, the ritual smashing of champagne bottles took place on the pavement outside the church.

Fullerton was a member of the blackshirted Fascist Mosleyite movement and was an admirer of Hitler, his gangs being ready to use their strong-arm methods in true storm-trooper style should the need arise. They had their political and religious ideologies mixed up, however, and instead of beating up Jews they would beat up Catholics which shows that their belief in a superior race was only another excuse for a show of power.

To his credit Fullerton also organised youth clubs of a sort and kept his boys fit and interested in sports but, of course, another motive for keeping his gang in the gym rather than the pub was to ensure their fitness in the pitched battles. Truces were called at New Year when there would be a spate of pub break-ins and drunken, naked 'Queens' would perform at parties for anyone who asked. On these occasions the leader of the Parlour Boys, James Dalziel or 'Razzle Dazzle' as he was colloquially known, only danced with other large male members of his gang, deeming it effeminate to dance with girls.

But even gang members and their molls have sentimentally long memories for at Fullerton's funeral in 1962 there were more than 300 mourners which, considering he was very much a spent force by that time, was a remarkable turn-out, the Orange Order being amply represented.

The ordinary policemen who had to control all this mayhem had their hands full. A typical example was Constable Roddie Gillies of the city's Eastern Division who, years later, described what one of those riotous occasions was like. "On the last Sunday in May each year the children in the East End became members of the Sacred Heart Chapel in Old Dalmarnock Road and the inauguration was celebrated by a procession of the children led by a junior pipe band from a Catholic school.

"On one of these occasions we were ordered to turn out in force in squad cars to Bridgeton Cross. When I got there the Cross was a battlefield. There was fighting everywhere and policemen were being chased onto tramcars.

"The juvenile pipe band was being escorted by men from Maryhill or the west end who had no experience of gang warfare and as they were being attacked by at least 500 Billy Boys they never had a chance.

"The first act of violence had been a brick through the big drum and this scattered the young band. My colleagues could not keep them together and had to run for their lives themselves.

"Just as I arrived Sergeant Robertson jumped out of another car and, as the Billies turned to attack us, we drew our batons and shoulder to shoulder we charged the gang and, despite their weapons, we laid out at least a dozen and the rest took to their heels when two police vans appeared.

"We rallied the pipe band and escorted them down to the chapel and then took the prisoners back to the police station where they were locked up.

"After they were locked up Inspector McPherson arrived and called me over.

"'I'm just back from Bridgeton Cross. It's really simmering and there is going to be a lot more trouble. Get a colleague and go there.'

"I got an older policeman, Hugh Jarvie, and we went back to the Cross. The place was indeed really simmering and so we had to be on our toes.

"We had not been there very long when a woman appeared with what she said was a stray child. She didn't really convince me but Hugh decided to take the little girl to the office.

"He wasn't far away when the trouble started. A double-decker bus was making its way slowly through the crowd from Dalmarnock towards London Road on its way to town. It had an open stairway to the top-deck, and it had not got clear when I heard a scream and saw a man running for his life after the bus with dozens of Billy Boys chasing him, all carrying knives or hatchets or some kind of offensive weapon.

"The leading gangster was carrying a butcher's knife and he was close to the man who made the bus but instead of diving inside he ran up the stair.

"His attacker did a hand balance on the rail and drove the knife into his back.

"I had been struggling through the crowd who were very obstructive and I only got there after the knife had been withdrawn. I laid the ned out and the knife fell out of his hand and was picked up before I could reach it.

"I went on one knee to stick the handcuffs on him, one of the gang gave the most vicious kick in the small of my back, it straightened me up and I saw his reflection in a mirror in the window opposite. He then tried to get past me to the bus but I laid him out and handcuffed him to his pal.

"I got them on to their feet and saw that the crowd were attacking the bus, throwing bricks through the windows.

"I shouted to the conductress to get away and take the injured man to hospital. They forced their way through the crowd and got away.

"I had a prisoner in each hand and started backing along London Road towards Tobago Street police station. The mob were throwing stones and bricks at me.

"When I was nearly opposite the part of Abercromby Street, I heard a voice, an Irish one, say, 'Can we help you, sir?' I turned around and saw two Irish boys as big as myself. 'Yes, you can help me,' I said, 'Take these two and I'll hold the mob back.' We got to the foot of Tobago Street when we met a rescue party from the office. A woman had ran there and told them I was in big trouble.

"When we got to the office there was, a call from Duke Street Hospital giving the name of the man who had been taken there by the bus driver and saying his condition was serious but he was expected to live.

"I charged the two neds with forming part of a riotous and disorderly crowd, with waving knives and bayonets and with assault.

"They were locked up and eventually appeared at the High Court where they were sentenced to two years hard labour.

"The sequel to the story as far as I was concerned came when I collapsed in the street all of two months later and couldn't get up. The large muscle that had been kicked that Sunday had jumped out of place and was pressing against my lung.

"When I came round in the Royal Infirmary I was told I would never walk again but would be on full pay for the rest of my life.

"I was eventually put into plaster and kept on my back for some weeks.

"The muscle healed back into place and I was back on duty in three months.

"When I had first regained consciousness a Sergeant at the Infirmary read a commendation from the Chief for bravery. 'They must have thought I was going to die,' I said. 'They weren't the only ones; the Infirmary doctor said."

Those were certainly tough days in which to be a policeman in Glasgow and the gang situation was getting so out of hand that successful crimebuster Sir Percy Sillitoe was brought from Sheffield to smash them. His methods were robust but worked. Using the roughest, toughest men of the force he would secrete them in furniture vans, converge on fights and let them have a free hand with whatever force they cared to use. This was in the days before such niceties as the Council for Civil Liberties and, even if the hooligans had understood their rights, the heavy squad, as they bludgeoned into them with fists, boots and batons, would not have been inclined to take much notice. Injuries sustained to accused hooligans were in court accredited to other gang members. Sillitoe was nicknamed 'Hitler' by his victims (which was ironic coming from Fuhrer worshipper Fullerton). But the fact remains that the gangs feared him because he was fighting them on their own terms and his methods were partially successful in that they forced gang warfare into decline and put offenders behind bars without, however, obliterating the problem. No great detective work was needed for these louts, simply brute force.

Sillitoe at the time he was Chief Constable (from 1931 to 1943) was idolised as the perfect policeman by the city's respectable citizenry. As well as gang busting, he brought in the fingerprint department, police boxes, diced police caps because they are easier to recognise in the dark and he introduced Glasgow's first marriage guidance council. He also started an intelligence force called the 'C' Specials, introduced radio cars and formed a river patrol. A dedicated Chief, hard but fair and a stern disciplinarian, he frequently dressed up as a workman and went round the city to check up on his own men. But he also went to the funerals of down and outs and paid for meals and drinks for those who turned up for the service without revealing who he was. His opinion of the gangs was succinct, "We are determined to fight gangsters with the utmost ferocity. These hooligans are merely unemployable louts. They find their courage in numbers. They are craven-hearted rats when alone. We are out to teach them that they must take heed of the law."

However, certain members of Glasgow Corporation lived to regret inviting him into the city. After he was finished smashing up organised hooliganism and imprisoning the violent leaders, Sillitoe turned his attention to graft rings within the Corporation. His plain clothes 'C' Specials eavesdropped on conversations in the back rooms of pubs where contractors gave over wads of notes to councillors in the building committees involved in carving up, demolishing and redeveloping the sprawling city. Several councillors ended up behind bars alongside the gangsters.

But like gang warfare Sillitoe was not able to stamp out graft which has plagued the city up to the present day. Old boy networks and corruption flourish just as easily among so-called socialist friends of the people, who have dominated the City Chambers for years, as among anyone else.

The first Chief Constable of Glasgow to be knighted, Sillitoe went on to become head of MI5 and died in 1962. But he always claimed his years as Glasgow's Chief were the happiest of his life, the most rewarding and most satisfying.

While Sillitoe was smashing the gangs someone else was making them immortal in a book. It is sad but typical that the best known, some would say notorious, and most read book about Glasgow is not a great work of art about beauty and nobility but is instead an arguably poorly written treatise on squalor and violence. The subject of *No Mean City* by A. McArthur and H. Kingsley Long is the razor gangs of the Gorbals and the characters, most of them exaggerated, are nevertheless based on real life. The conditions of massive overcrowding in evil smelling ghettoes are certainly not exaggerated. Written in suitably arid style by Mr. McArthur, a Gorbals grocer, when the longhand manuscript arrived on the desk of his publishers they were impressed by the book's power but appalled at its lack of literacy which is why a second writer, H. Kingsley Long, had to be brought in. The book became a bestseller, topping the million mark following its publication in 1956. Up to now it has sold more than 17 million copies.

It is sad but typical that Mr. McArthur gained little from this. He tried to write a sequel, *No Bad Money*, which would be a similar success (again with a co-writer) but it was a poor reflection of his first book. He subsequently took to drink because his confidence in any writing ability he might have had was shattered. He was finally found dead on the banks of the Clyde full of methylated spirits.

To add to the city's bad image, it is at least unfortunate that the picture conjured up by the name Glasgow was for many years abroad based on the brilliant caricature of a drunken, bunnetted Scottish working man portrayed by Will Fyffe leaning on a lamppost, bawling and slurring,

> *Ah belang tae Glesca, dear auld Glesca toon,*
> *But there's somethin' the ma'er wi' Glesca*
> *Fur it's goin' roon' an' roon',*
> *Ah'm only a common old workin' chap*
> *As anyone here can see*
> *But when Ah get a couple o' drinks on a Setterday*
> *Glasgow belongs to me!*

Will Fyffe, a Dundonian, paid only a few shillings for the song to an impoverished writer and then proceeded to make his fortune.

Sillitoe's ongoing campaign to clean up Glasgow was interrupted by the Second World War which helped his task enormously because it channelled the young Scots natural aggression into killing Germans instead of his fellow countrymen, just as the Great War had done.

The jocks have always had a proud military reputation since the

Napoleonic Wars and they were among the foremost in every campaign against the Nazis. Robert Graves was a trifle unkind when he said the Jock was the first soldier to run into battle and the first to run out, because many a commander was grateful he had the Scottish regiments to fling into the line where others wavered. Among the military cemeteries scattered throughout the world there are lying many who undoubtedly would have made up the ranks of armed gangs and come to a bad end. It was William Pitt the Younger's idea to channel the aggressiveness of the clan system, with its feuds and territorial squabbling and raiding, into organised regiments and it is interesting to note that an old clan map of Scotland resembles on a grand scale what a Glasgow gang map represents on a smaller scale. Perhaps history has only changed on the surface and the city has become a microcosm for a national tendency of banding together for mutual defence and attack.

Be that as it may, not even World War could wipe out the Glasgow gangs, as had previously been shown in 1914, and the domestic warfare continued uninterrupted although on a much reduced scale than in its heyday. The blackout was great fun for the teenagers not yet called up. The temptations of bombed or derelict houses where there could be cash, the tripping up and baiting of drunks in the black streets, the thrill of escaping down moonlit alleys, the real fireworks on Clydeside with the bombs blitzing the shipyards and the world gone mad with violence, and all of this with Dad away at the wars and Mum too busy coping with rationing and no discipline anywhere except from exasperated policemen with inefficient torches stabbing through the darkness.

After 1945 many young men had had their glut of violence. Many had their eyes and aspirations opened and widened to the world, thanks to military service. With horizons broadened and senses they never knew they possessed newly stimulated they were not prepared simply to slide back into the narrow, claustrophobic jungle of the closes where the next district could be the other side of the moon. Some simply emigrated, some decided to make a new kind of life for themselves well away from the threat of a criminal life. Most felt there was a social change in the air and there was. The huge, gaunt ghettoes were to be a thing of the past and the socialist brothers in the City Chambers were to bring in a New Order. Needless to say, it did not happen quite as envisioned.

Their good intentions cannot be doubted but that was not enough. The Labour-controlled Corporation idea was that because of the appalling slumlands choking up the city like cancer, an affront to modern man and a strangling grip on civilised development, there should be no less than a bulldozing blitzkrieg on these old areas and the inmates should be lifted and deposited en bloc in brand new dormitory estates on the virgin green fields fringing the city. The project and cost was colossal (as was the graft) and the estates were huge, cut off except for poor bus services from the city centre and virtually townships on their own. But townships without a heart.

While the Corporation were flinging up hundreds of miles of lookalike three storey, balconied rows of houses, admittedly cleaner than the slums and with indoor toilets and the luxury of baths, the planners forgot basic amenities which make society en masse tolerable. The new inhabitants of Easterhouse, Drumchapel, Pollok and Castlemilk in the East, North, West and Southern fringes found it even difficult to find nearby shops. And as for any form of entertainment or sport or public relaxation of any kind, a resolution of 1890 forbidding this on municipal housing estates put a real damper on the spirits of the people. There was no money to build places of entertainment anyway because the first priority was always houses, houses, houses. Glasgow was to be dragged screaming into the mid-twentieth century world of concrete and chrome by eager architects whether it squealed about it or not.

As word filtered through to the beleaguered areas to be demolished that all was not exactly paradise in the new estates, panic spread and inhabitants who loved the old areas in which they had been reared fought councillors, contractors, sometimes even police before being taken from their tenements, in some cases on the same day they were demolished. For all their obvious faults, the tenements were built in districts which had themselves been villages before being swallowed up by the city and they did have a community atmosphere. Everyone knew their neighbours, took their turn washing the stairs, cared for people when they were ill, went to the same weddings, parties, funerals, the same churches or chapels, the same schools, cinemas, pubs, dance halls, laundries or 'steamies', swimming baths, shops, football grounds, bookies. Doors were often left unlatched throughout the day for families and kids to come in and out at will. And yet those in authority made little attempt to keep this community spirit intact. Possibly many middle class professionals were not even aware it existed. People were only statistics and flung to the four winds regardless of friends, relatives or neighbours, leaving behind decimated or demolished areas with only the wind tip-toeing over what for all the world resembled bomb sites. What the Luftwaffe could not do the planners did with a vengeance. Throughout the late forties, fifties and early sixties this furious rehousing to far flung new schemes continued apace.

But even the misplaced enthusiasm of the planners could not cope with the problem. More than 80,000 new municipal houses were built between 1945 and 1968. And in the decade alone from 1958 more than 17,000 families were rehoused completely outwith the city boundary whereas more than 36,500 were given new homes in the 27 redevelopment schemes earmarked within the city. And yet one house in three was considered sub-standard by the mid-sixties. It has been a case of staggering from crisis to crisis with still no solution in sight. In the late sixties it was estimated Easterhouse had a population of more than 45,000 and Drumchapel only slightly less. Both had an unusually high number of teenagers, around 16% of the total population, who were aged between fifteen and nineteen and ripe for trouble.

The effect on street gang warfare of this upheaval was not at first apparent. Internecine fighting had continued since the thirties like a low grumbling volcano. Sons whose fathers and grandfathers had been tearaways could hardly be expected to turn into angels, although many did manage to improve themselves at the onset of what was briefly to be known as the affluent society. But apart from occasional eruptions the fighting was not an unusual phenomena and was one that could be contained.

It was with the widespread rehousing projects and the massive drifts in population within a restricted area that gang violence gradually began to increase. If youngsters felt it necessary to assert their individuality and identify themselves with a gang in an environment where they had amenities and where their parents were reasonably contented with their lot, how much more likely that they would feel the need to ventilate their aggression collectively in the housing deserts they now found themselves transported to and where there was nothing else to do but hang about and grumble, where the atmosphere, even at home, was one of boredom, depression and frustration.

And in the areas nearer the city that they left behind, the disruption and demolition turned communities into shell shocked ruins, where occasional tenements stood like giant dolls houses or where soulless high rise flats reared up like vast concrete tombs and where bitterness took once more to the streets, fed by the appalling ugliness and deprivation all around.

And so it was that in the late fifties the old Glasgow tradition of street gang violence, omnipresent and ever dormant, came back with a vengeance.

On the police charge sheets it read 'group disorders' but it was mass gangs fighting in the streets with greater viciousness, with more knives and weapons allied to a ruthless disregard for life or property.

At one stage the situation deteriorated to such an extent that the Royal Infirmary was running out of blood with which to transfuse victims.

One top surgeon let the public know exactly what was going on by stating that during one summer 950 cases of assault were dealt with by the casualty department and said his staff had also coped with 42 serious stabbings, the knife now having taken over from the razor as the weapon among the hoodlums who were mostly in their late teens or early twenties.

Newspaper reports of stabbings and gang fights, mostly at weekends, rose alarmingly throughout the early sixties and new gang names began to appear. The Tongs from Townhead, the Fleet from Maryhill, the Shamrock from Blackhill, the Cumbie from the inevitable Gorbals, the Govan Team, the Buck and the Drummie from Drumchapel, the Toi and the Young Team from Castlemilk, and a veritable vipers nest from Easterhouse including the Bal T'oi, the Bar L (named after Barlinnie Prison), the Torran Toi and so on.

One even more alarming aspect was the indiscriminate use of violence, not just against rivals but against society as a whole. In the past if an innocent passerby was assaulted by a gang it was normally in the furtherance of theft. But now pedestrians were being felled in the streets simply because they were there. Even girls standing looking in shop windows ran the risk of being literally stabbed in the back and it became a common occurrence for gangs high on cheap wine and pep pills to go running amok along the city streets at night, slashing out at anything that moved. These were truly children of the new schemes. A typical case which thankfully ended in a prison sentence was that of the leader of the Tongs who was sitting in a cafe in Parliamentary Road near Dundas Street Bus Station in the city centre when he boasted for a bet that he would leap on the first bus that came along and stab the first person he came across. He was as good as his word and the fact that the victim who died was an elderly cripple who had just been visiting his sister was irrelevant as far as the sacrificial act of killing for ego was concerned.

The gangs varied from groups of kids trying to act tough right through to real killers with little conscience and a hatred of society. One thing was certain, there were a great many more gangs and they were on the increase. A certain amount of affluence in the sixties which made them more independent of their parents was a contributory factor but basically it was the old aggression in a more virulent form.

Of course the more wild and outrageous the deeds the more the thugs laid themselves open to prosecution and the High Court dock began to fill up with the 'most mental' ones, those with the worst reputations, those who verged on the psychotic but who were looked up to with awe by the disturbed members of their teams. The judges were not at all in awe and led by Lord Cameron the sentences meted out became more swingeing.

However, there seemed to be more hooligans than police and Easter 1967 went into the annals as 'Bloody Easter' because there were twenty two stabbings in the city on the Friday and Saturday nights alone.

The tenants of Easterhouse wanted to form vigilante groups but were warned off this shortcut to anarchy by the senior magistrate. There were the parrot calls for bringing back capital and corporal punishment with the usual politicians jumping on the bandwagon. Shopkeepers and businessmen petitioned M.P.s for protection from vandalism. Figures revealed that in 1965 more than 850 people had been arrested for carrying offensive weapons and that more than 1,500 were arrested for breach of the peace and almost the same amount again for disorderly behaviour in connection with gang fights. To ease public alarm an anti-teenage gang committee was formed headed by the Lord Provost and Chief Constable.

In 1968 gang violence in Easterhouse hit the national headlines through an unusual source. Popular singer Frankie Vaughan who had done much to help boys clubs in England was asked by desperate locals in the East End if he would come to try and save the situation in Easterhouse. He made several flying visits and launched 'the Easterhouse Project', gaining much free publicity in the process. There was a weapons armistice for a day and an assortment of knives and bayonets were actually handed in by teenagers, but not as many as stayed in private hands and, anyway, they were replaceable. There were press conferences, lectures to schoolchildren, discussions with police, social workers and prison officers but at the end of it all the 'Easterhouse Project' deteriorated down to two rainlashed and slogan sprayed Nisson huts on a piece of waste ground used sporadically by teenagers. But many youth leaders poured a lot of energy into keeping their flock out of trouble and it aroused a lot of interest at the time although one cynical television comedian, remarking on a current spectacular Army action by Colonel Colin 'Mad Mitch' Mitchell against terrorists in Aden, suggested the Argyll and Sutherland Highlanders be parachuted into Easterhouse.

Several of the toughest gang members as they matured in the criminal fraternity left street fighting behind to go into organised crime, not just in their native city but throughout Britain. They were a respected lot and the favourite hirelings of mobs in London who knew they could be counted on to mix it with the most notorious.

The Kray twins used several specially flown-in criminals but even they were sometimes dismayed by the lack of sophistication and misplaced enthusiasm used to persuade victims when instead of ending in fear or bruising or cuts as well as cash the situation culminated in an unremunerative death. But other mobs and other cities had their quotas of Glaswegians who had decided to move on to other hunting grounds.

Thanks to the police once more getting tough, using flying support units to converge on battles, more sophisticated techniques in radioing for help, heavy sentences from the courts and, not least, the stupidity and reckless bravado of the gang members themselves in committing acts for which they were bound to get caught, the menace of the gangs controlling the streets was held at bay and once more subsided to a tolerable level. But it did not go away and just like the past hundred years there is no sign that it will do so.

There has been one dramatic change in the seventies and eighties compared to the past and that is one for the worse. The number of murders and serious assaults committed by gang members has increased. The reason for this is the indiscriminate, callous use of the knife in attacks rather than the use of the traditional, less lethal razors and bludgeons of the past. Ghastly as it is, a razor will disfigure before it will kill whereas once a knife has punctured a vital organ it results in death.

Although the scrap may not have started out as lethal, once it is all over a bloodied corpse can be lying in the gutter. It is ironic that while the actual number of weapon wielding gangs roaming the streets have decreased from the 'slashing sixties', when attacks occur now they are much more deadly because they involve knives being wielded by a hard core of potential murderers. It has always been an argument of the police force as regards stop and search powers that apart from any potential infringement of human rights they would possibly be saving a human life.

A thug who pockets a knife before going out on the streets is well aware he could kill so why not take it off him before he gets the chance is the way the argument runs - it is a perfectly valid one although it implies having trust in the police doing the searching.

Murders committed by gang members, outside any they might commit inside their family circle, are in two categories: firstly, against another hoodlum in a gang brawl and, secondly, against a complete outsider.

Two examples in the early summer of 1977 will illustrate them both. In Easterhouse yet again there was an arranged Friday night pitched battle between two drunken rival gangs using knives, swords and hatchets. One thug was isolated from his mates in the melee and blows were rained down on him by surrounding rivals. The battle was still going on when the ambulance arrived but it could not get through to the assaulted youth because his attackers had not finished their work.

The ambulance was attacked, its windows were smashed, the crew threatened and they had to beat a retreat, urgently summoning help by radio. By the time another ambulance and a squad car arrived the youth was dying from multiple stab wounds. This led to Easterhouse residents resurrecting plans for vigilante groups because of the breakdown of law and order, a situation not helped by Government spending cuts on the police. Periodic bus curfews against outlying districts as a protest against assaults on crews did not help matters either. This is a typical situation of lawlessness in the street leading to arbitrary death of a gang member.

The second totally callous type of murder can be exemplified by a case where a uniformed primary schoolboy and his pal were sitting in a park in Bishopbriggs, a middle class burgh outwith the city, drinking lemonade on their way back from school. Two older louts from a more low-life area passing by started some horseplay and one of the boys was forced to drink vodka before being stabbed once and fatally. Killer and victim never met before.

When the two thugs were finally traced one blamed the other and when the accused was found guilty and sentenced he shouted his gang slogan "Bison!" and gave a defiant salute. He no doubt thought he had proved himself a hard man to go down in the violent folklore of his area.

Chapter two:
THE PATRIOTIC CRACKSMAN

Great escaper, expert safeblower, decorated undercover agent, folk hero, athlete, rebel, villain – 'Gentle Johnny' Ramensky was all of these and one of the most colourful characters ever to emerge from the shadows of Glasgow's underworld. Throughout his long criminal career he was many things to many people while always remaining his 'own man'.

He was of a breed now virtually extinct: a criminal whom the public liked. As opposed to anonymous hooligans, he was every inch an individualist, one of those people who by some of their daring, often ridiculous, exploits bring some light and human warmth into the darkest of corners.

Johnny was born in Glenboig on the outskirts of Glasgow in 1905 the son of Lithuanian immigrants. His father, a coal miner, died when he was a child and his mother, who had lost an arm in an accident, had to bring up Johnny and his two sisters in a gloomy row of cottages where poverty was rife and the day's meal a crisis to be considered with every dawn. Johnny was left very much to his own devices and loved to get out into the country fields, away from the restrictions of home, where he excelled himself among his mates at athletics and football. His high spirited fitness marked him out as different from what he considered the grubby, rough company around him.

He left school at fourteen and, following the tradition of coalfields everywhere, took up his father's job down the mines. But the sparkling twenties somehow did not reach Lanarkshire where the depression struck early and miners were laid off or had their wages cut. The Ramensky family decided work prospects might be better in the city and moved into the Gorbals where many of their fellow Lithuanians and their descendants had settled to await the good life which was always just around the corner out of reach.

But unemployment in Glasgow was running at 30% at this time. Heavy industries had been the first to be hit by a worldwide recession. The unemployed took to the streets, socialist agitators addressed mass gatherings and the army and police had to disperse crowds of up to a hundred thousand.

The more passive unemployed spent their time playing dominoes in public halls or church halls or took part in organised country walks and hill climbs or in the reading rooms of public libraries or sitting about public parks. Johnny Ramensky was neither political nor passive so, like many others, he made a conscious decision. He looked around him, felt the holes in his pockets and decided if he could not make it to the top legitimately he would get there up the back stairs. He took to a life of crime.

By the time he was eighteen Johnny had come several times in contact with the law because of petty thieving. After two court appearances within a short space of time he was committed to Polmont Borstal near Falkirk. Pending his removal there he was required by statute to spend two months in solitary confinement at Barlinnie Prison which he loathed with all his heart and soul. But he found Polmont even worse. In those days it was the only borstal in Scotland and was staffed by officious, uniformed thugs who believed in putting in the boot and baton first and asking no questions at all. It toughened up young Johnny and he found nervous release in the compulsory physical fitness regime in the gym. He took out his frustration and anger in stretching his body's energies to the limit. Within months he was a keep-fit fanatic, a passion that was to remain with him throughout his life.

Five feet seven inches tall, he had extremely strong musclebound arms and was stockily built with fair hair and a hardened, bitter face. His keep-fit regime meant no smoking and throughout his life he never drank spirits although he enjoyed an occasional stout.

When he came out of the Polmont breeding ground of young prematurely hardened criminals Johnny returned to his tenement home in the Gorbals but conditions were no better and now, with the added burden of a criminal record, he found it impossible to get work. Along with another borstal boy named Tommy whom he had befriended in Polmont, he decided it was the moment to move into the big time. They became safe blowers.

An incentive for Johnny to make money quickly had come from the realms of romance. He had fallen in love with a pert, lively neighbourhood girl called Daisy McManus and after a brief, passionate courtship they became engaged.

In the late twenties and early thirties there were very few expert safe blowers in Britain, probably not more than ten. Of these the majority were from Glasgow and the surrounding area. Johnny, with his early apprenticeship in explosives down the pits, became a quick learner and even taught some of the older hands a few tricks. Tommy was also an adept cracksman, having learned at the hands of the top man, 'Scotch Jimmy', who he had shared a cell with in Barlinnie.

Johnny and Tommy roamed far and wide and the pickings were good for in those days a few hundred pounds was a fortune. They became known as a good team in the underworld and inevitably the police got to hear.

On his illicit earnings Johnny married his Daisy and for a while it was all wine and roses. But one night the police raided their happy home and Johnny was arrested after one of his safe cracking sorties and jailed for several years.

It was while he was in Peterhead Prison in 1934 that Johnny was summoned to the Governor's office and told that criminal life's harsh realities had taken their toll of his bright bride and that she had collapsed and died of a heart attack. Shattered, Johnny immediately applied for permission to attend the funeral. This was refused. The model prisoner up until then, he now decided to escape, if only to stand at the plot where Daisy was buried and say a quiet prayer.

One night shortly after midnight he dipped a small wire he had filched into the door lock of the hospital wing where he had been put because of chronic depression, stole across the courtyard and, using his physical fitness to the full, scaled the high, crenelated prison gate and hung by his fingertips on the other side before dropping to freedom.

But once clear of the prison there was still 170 miles to Glasgow and no previous escaper had ever succeeded in getting south of the River Don Bridge at Aberdeen some thirty miles from the prison. Indeed few escapers had ever succeeded in getting south of the bridge at Ellon, only some fifteen miles from the prison. Anyone going south had to cross these two bridges above treacherous and fast flowing rivers and it was naturally at these points that the police always set up their road blocks.

Such was the case on the occasion of Johnny's first escape and shortly after daybreak he was caught trying to cross the bridge at Ellon in the back of a lorry. On being returned to prison he was placed in the punishment block where he was shackled to the cell wall. The news that he was being held in chains reached the outside world and an M.P. travelled to the prison to protest at such barbarity. As a result the chains were removed and Johnny had the dubious distinction of being the last prisoner in Scotland to be shackled.

On his eventual release, Johnny returned to his old haunts and now, with Daisy gone (he had promised her he would go straight when he got out), there was no compunction to give up his life of crime. He and his pal Tommy returned to safe blowing.

But by the time the Second World War broke out Johnny was back in Peterhead serving five years for blowing an Aberdeen baker's safe.

It was in 1942, two months before his sentence was due to expire, that Johnny received a mysterious visitor, one who had come all the way from the War Office in London to talk about safe blowing. Johnny was taken under military escort to Whitehall where in a subterranean room he was told his criminal expertise was to be used in the fight against Nazi Germany.

After signing a document agreeing to join the armed forces, Johnny was escorted back to Peterhead because the law had to be obeyed first - war or no war - and he impatiently sat out the remaining weeks of his sentence.

On his release he was taken to a special training camp where he was put through a tough commando course, a fitness test which Johnny revelled in, tuning his body like tempered steel and taking on the toughest tests with comparative ease. He was taught how to use more sophisticated explosives and, much to his amusement, was requisitioned a number of safes to practise with. When his special training was complete Private Johnny Ramensky in red beret and uniform, was promoted to the rank of sergeant and assigned to a crack commando unit.

Much of his wartime activity is shrouded in mystery but several facts are known. He was parachuted several times behind enemy lines in order to get into designated enemy premises and blow safes to acquire secret papers and military plans. After D-Day Johnny and his unit took over enemy army posts far in advance of the front line and Johnny would crack safes while his comrades held off the enemy until reinforcements arrived. When the Allies invaded Rome it was his unit which took over the foreign embassies and on one day alone Johnny blew fourteen safes. It was also in Italy that he was a witness to an atrocity when his unit over-ran an S.S. outpost. The young Aryans with the death's head insignia were separated from the Wehrmacht soldiers, taken outside and cursorily shot. Johnny was asked if he wanted to take part but, detesting bloodshed, declined. When the Allies stormed Reichsmarshal Goering's palatial estate at Karinhall in the Schorfhleide it was Johnny who blew the pompous, bewildered drug addict's safes.

When hostilities ended Johnny was given the Military Medal for his war services and found himself with an ill-fitting suit of clothes back in civvy street. But after his heady days with the commandoes, he found it difficult to adjust to what he considered dull normality. He met up with Tommy again and before long they were back at their old trade, Johnny having gained additional expertise due to his war services.

In the North of England they were caught in the act after a particularly loud explosion and Tommy was given seven years whereas Johnny, because of his outstanding war record, was let off with five. He was returned to the familiar grey walls of Peterhead and after serving three years and four months he was released. But not for long. Soon he was back emptying safes, again he was caught and again the High Court decided to be lenient - five years.

During his brief spell of liberty Johnny had met and fallen in love with an attractive widow from the Gorbals, Mrs. Lilly Mulholland, and once more he started to entertain thoughts of going straight.

But like most of his kind Johnny's idea of going straight was something you did after the 'Big Haul'. Money, quickly achieved and enough of it, was the criteria when it came to building a new future. During his spell in prison he hit on the idea that maybe he could earn enough legitimately by writing his memoirs. This was easier said than done because prison rules forbid the writing of autobiographies. But Johnny had the solution - he would write the outline of his memoirs secretly then escape to find a publisher. In 1952 with the manuscript of his life story tucked inside his shirt Johnny once more went over the wall at Peterhead.

This escape made front page news and, again because of his war record, the editorials were more sympathetic than condemnatory. The public was beginning to adopt him as an unlikely folk hero who was challenging the oppressive post war authorities and Johnny was rather inappropriately compared to Errol Flynn acrobatically escaping from the Sheriff of Nottingham's castle.

His second escape ended like the first and, still clutching the school exercise books which contained his life story, he was recaptured at the Bridge of Ellon by the same police officer who had caught him at the same spot previously. The news of his capture served to increase public sympathy and in the punishment block at Peterhead Johnny was swamped by letters from well wishers including an offer of marriage from a lady of means who offered him a life of ease and security. Although attracted by such an offer, Johnny wrote a polite refusal. His heart was with Lilly in her Gorbals flat.

In 1955 the gates of Peterhead were once again opened to allow him to walk free. On returning to Glasgow he and Lilly were married. Johnny typed his memoirs out but his literary plans came to nothing because his wartime exploits were covered by the Official Secrets Act and the Ministry of Defence refused to allow publication.

Later that summer Johnny and two other Glasgow criminals raided the British Linen Bank at Oban. They blew open the strongroom and two inner safes. They got away with £8,000 of the Bank's money plus deposit boxes and jewellery. His share of the booty would have been enough to set him up in business but within only a few months enough of it had gone to make this impossible. Johnny's greed and the desire to double the money had ruined his plans and fattened the wallets of several bookmakers.

Within weeks of this the public was reading press reports that Johnny Ramensky was once more in custody, this time for a raid on a bank in Rutherglen. Lilly, the bride of only a few months, was, like her predecessor, shattered when a policewoman appeared at her door to tell her the news.

Once again Johnny stood up in the dock at Glasgow High Court. The judge was Lord Carmont, notorious for the severe sentences he handed down. Johnny, conscious of the terrible pain he had caused Lilly, literally got down on his knees in the dock to plead for mercy but Lord Carmont was not the sort of man to fall for that kind of stuff.

He frowned sternly down at Johnny and declared, "You have been given chance after chance because of your war record. This time there will be no mercy. You will go to prison for ten years".

To Johnny this was totally unacceptable. He was serving the same sentence as a murderer or child rapist. For him it simply was not on. The public was not at all taken aback when once again the Press blazoned the news in 1958 that 'Gentle Johnny' had escaped from Peterhead. Twice more during the same year he succeeded in getting over the wall and always the result was predictably the same - recapture at the Bridge of Ellon, although he nearly made it clear the third time with a bit of inside help.

This plan of escape was not his own. It was thought up by another prisoner,'Darky' Davidson, who worked as the cleaner in the prison hospital. 'Darky' had an interest in locks through his profession of burglary and by a process of trial and error he succeeded in making a replica of a prison master key. Then he rolled back the heavy carpet in the doctor's office and prised up a couple of floorboards and showed Johnny where there was enough space for a full grown man to hide comfortably. This was the great escapee's domicile for the next few days. When the appointed time came, Johnny disappeared from the exercise yard. The alarm was raised. Up went the police cordons in the surrounding area and a special watch was kept on the Bridge of Ellon where the wife of one of the policemen, assuming the predictable, prepared a hot meal for Johnny.

After a few days in hiding he went over the wall. This tine he did not even get as far as the Bridge of Ellon. He was following the road south when a bus full of passengers went by and, because of the press publicity, he was recognised. The driver of the bus flagged down a police car and Johnny was recaptured once more. He offered no resistance thus living up to his nickname 'Gentle Johnny'. After his usual cup of tea at the police station he was returned to prison.

The general public feeling for him led to the actor Roddy McMillan writing a song, *Set Ramensky Free*, and this was recorded and sold well while Labour M.P. Norman Buchan jumped on the bandwagon by writing *The Ballad of Johnny Ramensky* which also became popular.

But despite all this sentimentality it was 1964 before Johnny was eventually released and by then he was almost sixty. Promises of employment made to him by businessmen while he was inside came to nothing on his release. He took a job as a labourer but within months of his release he stood in Paisley Sheriff Court and admitted breaking into Woolworth's Store in the town's High Street and attempting to blow a safe. He was only given two years and this surprised him so much that he staggered and said to the Sheriff, "Thank you very much, Sir, thank you."

But he was now at a stage in life where giving him a chance meant nothing. He was too old to make a fresh start. No sooner was he released than he was in trouble again.

On the night of January 3rd, 1967, two constables patrolling in Rutherglen to the south of the city were blown onto their backs by a blast from a bank in the Main Street which also shattered several windows. Surprised and a bit stunned they picked themselves up and, after investigating, they saw a shadowy figure drop nimbly from the bank roof and race off. They gave chase but it took them all their time, a rugby tackle and some fisticuffs to catch and hold the figure who turned out to be Johnny.

It turned out that not only had he used a ludicrously excessive amount of gelignite on the safe (which was empty) but in the process had contrived to ignore a drawer at his side which contained £80,000.

At the subsequent trial Johnny willingly pleaded guilty to the safeblowing charge but stubbornly refused on principle to plead guilty to a lesser charge of police assault. He protested angrily that he had never assaulted anyone in his life, hence the nickname 'Gentle', and had only been defending himself against two over-enthusiastic young constables. The jury believed him and he was quite delighted that his reputation remained untarnished on this point, even although he was given four years on the safe blowing charge.

By the end of that time he was nothing like the athlete he had once been. His age and the years in prison had worn him down to a shell of his former robust self and he was now a sad caricature, snowy haired and deeply furrowed. But he would never acknowledge that he was finished.

On one nocturnal foray into an office building, he shouted to his accomplice that he was having great difficulty trying to get a safe open using welding equipment. Johnny was on a lower floor of the building while his accomplice was rifling a safe upstairs. The second man eventually became fed up with Johnny's complaints and decided to have a look for himself. He found the cracksman had been trying to open the boiler used for heating the building.

In July 1970 he was again in court, this time for trying to blow the strongroom of the Burgh factors in Stirling. In making his way over the roof of the building he had slipped and fallen into the street where he could only lie suffering from severe injuries which only helped emphasise he was not the Ramensky of old. He was in hospital for fourteen weeks and on his discharge was sentenced to two years.

On his release he was shortly after charged with being on the roof of a shop in Ayr at midnight and given twelve months. It was to be his final sentence for while serving it Johnny made his final escape - in a wooden box. He collapsed in Perth Prison and died shortly afterwards in hospital.

Hundreds attended his funeral in St. Francis Chapel in the Gorbals, including all the notable characters of the underworld not in prison, a send-off befitting a villain who, for all his misdeeds, had captured the public imagination.

Chapter three:
WOLF AT THE DOOR

Scotland's worst murderer was a loner, an enigma to most people who knew him, a creature who roamed on nights of the full moon creating in the confines of his ego-centric personality a sense of power and omnipotence, a feeling that he could toy with peoples lives and deaths. He was highly intelligent but always self centred and boastful. He was goodlooking and graceful with a slim but strong body, wicked eyes which could freeze over like the black marble of tombstones, an aquiline face with jet-black, brushed-back hair. He was a criminal who was yet never really part of that shadowy fraternity because there was always something icy about him deep down which could not merge with his fellows and it was the underworld which helped to eventually put him down. He was attractive to women yet was humiliatingly impotent at the crucial moment and could lapse into fearful outbursts of temper or sullen moods and at such times he was as unfathomable as the dark waters of a still loch. He took a psychotic delight in the phallic handling of guns which enhanced his powers of destructiveness. His name was Peter Thomas Anthony Manuel.

He was born in Manhattan, New York in 1927. The family who had emigrated decided the New World was not up to their expectations and returned to the old country in 1932 where they went back to Motherwell, Lanarkshire, before moving to Coventry. It was here that the rebellious adolescent who never could do what he was told first broke the law at the age of twelve. He was put on probation for burglary and only five weeks later, having sneeringly turned his back on this warning, was sent to an approved school for an identical offence. Here he was nothing if not dedicated in his determination to get out - eleven times he escaped and was recaptured in three years. While on the run he invariably committed more thefts to keep himself in funds and on one housebreaking expedition he assaulted an occupant with a hammer. Just before Christmas 1942 he robbed and indecently assaulted the wife of a school employee. In March 1943 he ended up in borstal, which he did not escape from, and on his release two years later he rejoined his family in Viewpark, Uddingston, Lanarkshire, where they had moved following the Coventry Blitz. On a visit to Blackpool he was acquitted on a charge of burglary.

The important years of puberty and adolescence had therefore been spent in hard, oppressive, all male institutions or on the run where self reliance and survival and his own considerable resourcefulness were the priorities of the day. There was no stabilising influence of home, no love, no guidance, no reassurance, no praise, no encouragement. He was a public enemy from very early on and he knew it and revelled in it. As far as he was concerned he was the underdog who was going to become top wolf.

And on his return to Lanarkshire from Blackpool he was involved in a series of incidents which were to seal his fate.

It began on the night of 3rd of March 1946. A Mrs. K. was walking along a quiet, deserted footpath between Mount Vernon Avenue and North Carrick Drive on the eastern outskirts of Glasgow verging on Lanarkshire. She had her three-year-old daughter with her as she stepped through the unlit dark. Suddenly a shadowy figure sprang at her from some bushes and dragged her down an embankment. But she screamed and fought off her attacker who scrambled up the embankment and ran off.

The woman later gave a vague description to the police and, because of this and his record and the fact that he was local, suspicion fell on Manuel. They called at his home the next day but he had gone away.

Four nights later in the same area a young nurse returning from the local hospital was attacked. She was carrying a suitcase and walking along a lonely, dark road when a figure sprang on her and hauled her into a hedge. But her screams were heard by a motorcyclist who was passing and he stopped his machine. The attacker once more took to his heels with his business unfinished. The brief description the nurse could give to the police again fitted Manuel.

The following night at around the same time - 9.30 - the third victim was attacked in the same area. A Mrs. M. was on her way home along a deserted road when she was pounced upon from behind. The assailant first beat her then forced her in a state of shock to walk along the road towards an overhead railway bridge where he forced her through a barbed wire fence and down an embankment. He tore off her dress and raped her.

Later Mrs. M. struggled back up to the road where, in a distraught state of collapse, she met a pedestrian. Again the description of the attacker fitted Manuel but it was a vague one as in the two previous cases.

The next day Manuel was taken into custody and an identification parade was held at which all three women attended. The young nurse and Mrs. K. picked out Manuel but Mrs M. who was the only one who had actually been raped and who had spent the longest time with her attacker, failed to pick him out.

At the time of the attacks Manuel was on £60 bail after being charged with a break-in at a bungalow the previous month. This was the first time he had been charged in Scotland and shortly after the identification parade he was found guilty of this break-in and fourteen other similar offences for which he was given a sentence of twelve months. With their suspect safely locked up the police, and more particularly the forensic department, meticulously investigated the rape of Mrs. M. The evidence they came up with was the cast of a shoe heel found at the scene which matched a pair of shoes belonging to Manuel and specks of dust and red sandstone from the ground in the area of the attack matched particles found on his clothing. And although Mrs. M. had failed to pick him out her description of the attacker was still similar to Manuel.

The Procurator Fiscal decided not to bring Manuel to trial for all three attacks but only for the one where, ironically, the victim had failed to identify him. His subsequent conviction was due almost entirely to forensic evidence and he was sentenced to eight years.

In his defence it must be said that there was nothing unusual about his shoes or their size and that particles of dust and red sandstone are common throughout the whole of Lanarkshire.

Throughout these long years in prison Manuel brooded and kept very much to himself. Any conversation with fellow prisoners inevitably led to him reiterating time and again that he was entirely innocent of the rape charge. He boasted he would get the police back for what they had done to him and spent long hours dreaming up schemes of revenge.

His anger and frustration took itself out on the only form of uniformed authority around - the 'screws'. As a newly sentenced prisoner he was required to spend the first three days in solitary. This was so that the staff could keep him under strict observation and report to the prison medical officer if he was showing signs of mental disorder or suicidal tendencies. During this period he was not allowed cigarettes. One prison officer on looking through the judas hole of Manuel's cell saw him puffing away arrogantly. On opening the cell door to demand that he give up the cigarette, the officer saw Manuel flick it under his bed. Foolishly the officer stooped to retrieve it and Manuel aimed a savage kick in his face, the officer fell in a heap and Manuel put the boot in with a vengeance. Screams brought reinforcements, the prisoner was overpowered and that night received the beating of his life from Barlinnie's 'batter squad'. Twelve months was added to his sentence.

At Peterhead he again attacked a prison officer, this time with a steel food tray. He was sent to the segregation top security unit, known as the 'snake pit'.

As the years passed he wrote to lawyers about his innocence but no-one would take on his case. All appeals to authority came to nothing. Whether he was innocent of the rape is something that will never be known. What is fact is that shortly after he gave up the fight to clear his name he set out on a course that was to cost lives and cause a great deal of embarrassment, bafflement and consternation to the police who had sent him away. That he should have committed so many crimes in that particular area certainly strengthens the theory held by many criminals that his atrocities were his psychotic way of hitting back at the police. If he was in fact innocent of the rape charge the stigma attached to this would have been doubly hard to bear if, even at that stage of his life, he suffered the impotency of his later years and was incapable of raping anyone. The psychological wound throughout these dark years behind bars would have deepened and festered and have become such an ineradicable part of his vicious soul as to be virtually incurable. To say he was simply a psychopath with no regard for human life is too facile an explanation for the unusual nature of his crimes.

One of his first moves after his release was to go to Superintendent James Hendry of Lanarkshire Police to whom he strenuously claimed that he was innocent of the rape and he accused certain police officers of framing him but his allegations were cursorily dismissed.

He now mapped out in his head a very clear plan of where his hunting ground would be, his very own topography of terror, where he would stalk and seek his prey in a macabre act of revenge. His county of murder, Lanarkshire, had to be narrowed down to heighten the terror. His hunting ground was to stretch from Mount Vernon, a salubrious suburb on the south eastern outskirts of Glasgow to nearby residential Burnside and from there to the town of East Kilbride and back to his base headquarters in Uddingston, an area of a few square miles.

Shortly after his release he took up with a pretty bus conductress from Carluke, Anne O'Hara, and after a few months courtship they became engaged and the wedding was fixed for July 1955. Then, because he could not keep up with the sexual side of the relationship, Manuel had second thoughts. But instead of simply breaking off the engagement he perversely penned an anonymous letter to his fiance detailing his criminal past and Ann took the initiative in promptly calling the whole thing off.

Again perversely, on July 30th - the date when he had planned to marry - Manuel terrorised a woman with a knife.

Towards midnight the screams of a woman were heard to come from Lucie Brae near Birkenshaw. It was a quiet, warm summer night and several people heard the screams, two patrolling constables among them. They made a quick search of the area but found nothing suspicious. While this was going on a young woman named Mary McLauchlan, a 29-year-old weaver who came from Birkenshaw, was lying in a field with a knife pointed at her throat. She had been returning from a dance in Blantyre when she had been attacked by the man who now lay over her. The man detained her in the field all night but made no attempt to rape her. At one point, when he lit a cigarette, the woman recognised him in the sudden flare of the match although she did not know his name. She had seen him on the bus when she went to work in the mornings sitting chatting to an older man.

Next day the woman went to the police and later picked out Manuel's photograph. He was arrested within twenty-four-hours.

The trial was in October of that year at Airdrie Sheriff Court and Manuel the showman came into his own. He successfully defended himself, showing an adroitness and expertise in legal matters which enforced the opinion that many people always had of him that his quicksilver brain and eloquent talents were wasted in the world of criminality and, with the proper dedication and psychological outlook, could have been successfully channelled into another profession than that of violence. Certainly Manuel knew he was a cut above the ordinary crook and his success as a barrack room lawyer enhanced his already swollen ego.

The jury at Airdrie brought in a verdict of 'Not Proven'. In his defence Manuel had claimed that he and the woman had been courting and that the incident took place at noon not midnight. He claimed he had struck her earlier and that afterwards they had gone to the field accompanied by his Alsatian dog and that he had thrown the knife at the dog when it had gone too near the railway lines. He had failed to find the knife after this. The story was a blatant lie but the jury, not knowing of his record, decided to take the easy way out and Manuel walked free.

Cocksure of himself, Manuel now set off on a grim trail. On the afternoon of January 4th 1956 a labourer named George Gribbon was on the golf course at East Kilbride looking for lost golf balls when he saw in a hollow what appeared to be the body of a woman lying face down. He thought it might be a drunk woman taking a nap or sleeping it off but as he got nearer he saw that the skull had been badly injured and that she appeared to be dead. Mr. Gribbon hurried to find help and came upon three men working on a new road. When he told them what he had seen they seemed to think he was joking or mistaken and told him to shove off. Mr. Gribbon then hurried to nearby Calderglen Farm and the police were phoned. Meanwhile the three sceptical roadworkers had second thoughts about the matter and went to look for the body. When they found it they dropped their picks and shovels in horror and rushed to a nearby house and once more the police were telephoned.

The dead girl, seventeen-year-old Anne Knielands, had suffered a terrible death. Her skull had been smashed into fifteen pieces. She had been murdered on the night of January 2nd and her body had lain undiscovered in the hollow until the 4th. The signs found at the scene of the crime suggested that she had tried to run from her attacker. Her body had been lacerated with barbed wire in a frantic dash to escape. On the night she died a Mr. Hugh Marshall, out walking his dogs, heard a cry around 8.30 p.m. He later described it as a squealing kind of cry.

The dead girl's knickers had been ripped off, her clothes were in disarray and one of her nylons was also missing but there was no sign of any sexual attack.

Manuel came into this case at the beginning and in a very strange way. Police Constable Marr, one of the first officers to arrive on the scene, was despatched to trace Mr. Gribbon. On the way to Calderglen Farm, P.C. Marr spoke to a man who was in charge of a group of gas board workers. This man, Mr. Corrins, was in the company of Manuel at that moment. From Mr. Corrins P.C. Marr obtained a description of Mr. Gribbon who had passed them by. In the course of the conversation Manuel said to P.C. Marr, "What if this Gribbon doesn't want to come along? Can we punch him on the nose?" P.C. Marr, who did not know Manuel, noticed he had a number of scratches on his nose and right cheek.

Ten days after the murder, Manuel was interviewed by his old adversary Superintendent Hendry, as were his parents. His alibi was simple: he had never left home on the night of the murder. As for the scratches, he had received them in a fight in Glasgow but he could give no details about the man he had fought with and as for the scratches being inconsistent with a fight he said he found that highly debatable.

The murder investigation came to nothing and Manuel remained on the prowl until the night of March 23rd of that year. The police, acting on a tip-off, waited at Hamilton Colliery to capture two men who intended to break into the canteen. When they appeared around midnight one was captured on the spot. The other, Manuel, outran the police but he had been recognised and was arrested at home in the early hours of the morning. When he appeared in court he was granted bail and his trial was fixed for October.

But the threat of imprisonment did not deter him. On July 28th the police at Uddingston received a call that two men were acting suspiciously at the rear of a house and when squad cars converged two men were seen to jump from a wall and run off. One got away and one was caught. The first was Manuel and the second, his accomplice, Joe Brannan. Despite hours in the interview roam Joe kept his mouth shut about who had been with him which raised him in Manuel's eyes to a position of trustworthiness. This was to have important repercussions later on.

But it was two weeks before his trial that Manuel really showed his teeth once more. The plan was to break into the house of Mr. William Watt at number 5 Fennsbank Avenue, Burnside, where Manuel and a second villain hoped to steal a large sum of money after tying up the occupants. The accomplice was not aware of what Manuel's other intention was but the two agreed they would break into number 18 before raiding the Watt home.

A few days previously Mr. Watt had gone off on a fishing holiday taking with him his black labrador, Queenie. Mrs. Watt was not in good health and suffered from a heart complaint. On the night of the break-in her sister, Margaret Brown, came to the house to spend a night or two with her. Around 11.30 that night the Watt's daughter, sixteen-year-old Vivienne, came in from the house next door where she had been with her friend Deanne Valente.

From the house at number 18, which they knew would be empty, Manuel and his accomplice had a modest haul: a few rings, some clothing and some cash. In the early hours the pair made their way to number 5. Entry was gained by breaking a pane of glass in the front door and inserting a hand to turn the lock in the inside.

Both men entered the dark house and crept along the hallway. Manuel went first and disappeared into the room where Mrs. Watt and her sister were asleep. The accomplice moved towards the room where Vivienne was sleeping. As he turned the door handle he heard a loud bang come from the other room. He froze. Then there was another bang. At this Vivienne appeared at the door and, in an instinctive panic, the man punched her, connecting with the left side of her chin. Vivienne slumped unconscious to the floor. The man picked her up and placed her on the bed then ran into the room where the two bangs had come from. Manuel stood with a smoking revolver at the bedside, grinning. When the horrified accomplice saw the two women lying dead on their pillows, mouths agape, the blood trickling onto their nightdresses, he turned without a word and fled out of the house and the district as fast as his legs could carry him.

Manuel entered Vivienne's room and as she started to come round calmly shot her in the head as he had the two other women. But the girl did not die immediately. She was to linger on as if waiting to be discovered so that she could say something.

The nightdresses of the three were disturbed and they were placed in humiliating positions with their legs open but there were no signs of sexual molestation.

Not knowing if his accomplice might go to the police, Manuel decided to leave the house rather than search it for money or valuables. But he did pause for a few minutes to revel in the feeling of power the shootings had given him.

Mrs. Watt had a home help who was first to arrive on the scene but despite knocking on doors and windows she could not get in. It was the postman who realised something was seriously wrong when he saw the smashed panel. He used the same method of entry as the intruders and he was the first to discover the horror. Vivienne, who was still moaning when the postman found her, died as the ambulance was on its way. She had not managed to utter a word.

Forensic experts found a fairly fresh cigarette end and a spent match on the carpet of Vivienne's bedroom and the police quickly established that nothing had been stolen. The break-in at number 18 was discovered by a neighbour. It was found the place had been ransacked, someone had been lying on one of the beds with dirty boots and a tin of tomato soup had been spilled on one of the carpets.

In the small hours of the following morning detectives raided the Manuel house and despite an intensive search and lengthy interviews not only with Manuel but with the whole family they drew a blank. They did not press their enquiries because they felt they had a better suspect - Mr. Watt.

However, one man who was certain Manuel was the culprit was Chief

Inspector Muncie of the Lanarkshire force. On the day the murders had been discovered he had received a telephone call from one of his contacts in the underworld. The informant said that the previous evening he had been in Manuel's company drinking in a hotel. Manuel had told him that on that very night he was going to a wealthy house to rob it of a stack of money and, tapping his pocket where there was something bulky, he had added that he had the right thing for anyone who caught him at it. The informant had assumed he was talking about a gun. In the course of this conversation Manuel had boasted that he had tested the gun by shooting a cow dead in a field. He had shot it up the nostril. By a curious coincidence this rang a bell with Muncie. While on top of a bus in the Viewpark area he had seen a cow lying dead in a field. As a senior officer in the county force he was also an Inspector under the Diseases of Animals Act and had ensured that the cow had been examined for anthrax. The vet reported that there was no sign of anthrax but while he thought the animal might have died from stomach staggers he had noted bleeding from one of the nostrils and now agreed that the animal might have been shot although it had not crossed his mind at the time. It was now a race against time to try and trace the carcass and find the bullet. But the police were out of luck. The carcass was by this time in the local abattoir inside a boiling vat. But even here the police, in their determination to nail Manuel, did not give up. It took them four days to empty and search the vat but again they drew a blank.

Another informant told them that Manuel had also tested the gun by firing it into a tree near his home. The police methodically examined all the trees in the Viewpark area but again luck was with the killer and no bullet was found.

In checking out all the recent break-ins in the area Muncie found that one house had been broken into the night before the Watt murders. This was at Douglas Drive in Bothwell. The housebreaker had opened a tin of pears, drunk the juice and scattered the pears on the carpet similar to what had happened to the tomato soup at Fennsbank Avenue the following night. Curiously enough not much of value had been stolen but, among the articles that were, an unusual type of electric razor stood out as identifiable. Another curious aspect was that a mattress had been slashed and a watch belonging to one of the occupants inserted into it for no apparent reason. Closer investigation would have found a much smaller object - a spent bullet. Manuel had broken in and fired his gun into the mattress to rehearse the slaughter scheduled for the following night. Tragically, the bullet was not discovered until nineteen months had elapsed.

The police, under daily public pressure, now tried to build up their case against Mr. Watt. Unlike the other suspect, Manuel, who they were now - with one or two exceptions - inclined to eliminate from their inquiries, Mr. Watt had no record and was a prosperous and decent member of society. He was a master baker who owned a string of shops, was a respected Freemason and had a distinguished record in the Police War Reserve. But eleven days after the murders he was arrested and charged with having committed them.

There is no doubt that Mr. Watt, who was totally innocent, came perilously close to being hanged. Again doubtful identification played its part.

A week before the murders he and his dog had gone to the Cairnbaan Hotel in Lochgilphead for a fishing holiday. He had motored down the Loch Lomond

Road, a distance of ninety miles. Each night he telephoned his wife and on the eve of the murders he told her he was enjoying the rest and wanted to have an extra few days if that was okay with her and she agreed. He then sat and had a drink with the proprietor of the hotel who was an old friend, letting Queenie the labrador out for a run around midnight. On retiring for the night he said he would be getting up at 5.30 a.m. to go fishing and to this end borrowed an alarm clock. But it was not until 7.30 that he got up and to fill in the time till breakfast he had gone out to have a look at the water. At 8.30 a.m. he returned to the hotel, had breakfast and set out to do a days fishing. Two and a half hours later there was a telephone call from his brother. On returning to the hotel and being told the news, he collapsed, weeping. He was in such a state that it was agreed that a friend should go with him as far as Alexandria where Sergeant William Mitchell, an officer of the Lanarkshire force, was to pick him up. On the way to Alexandria Mr. Watt managed to pull himself together. He had once been a member of the police force himself and wanted to show a digni-fied, manly front. He even managed to pull a brave smile when he met the sergeant. It would have been better for him if he had remained weeping. Mitchell was later to state, "I went to Alexandria thinking I was bringing back a bereaved and broken man. What did I find? A man with a smirk on his face and without a tear."

In all their investigations the police heard from numerous people, barmen, hoteliers and friends of the family as well as business partners, that Mr. Watt had been devoted to his family. But he had to admit to being unfaithful to his wife on several occasions which, considering his wife's weak condition, was no heinous sin for a man still with healthy appetites. But at no time was a mistress found. There was no-one special in the background.

The police theory was that Mr. Watt had crept surreptitiously out of the hotel with his dog without disturbing anyone in the early hours, drove to Glasgow, murdered his family then drove back to the hotel for 7.30.

Long distance lorry drivers were interviewed and all garages were checked to see if he had filled up with petrol, without success. Then the alarm clock took on a sinister significance. The bell on the clock only rang for a couple of seconds before shutting itself off but the theory was that if he had been in his room as he said then this should have wakened him up. But a middle aged man who had been out in the fresh air a lot and had also been drinking could easily sleep through a two sec-ond alarm and, even if he had woken up, could easily have gone back to sleep again.

The time taken to do the Lochgilphead-Glasgow trip was checked. Mr. Watt said that at night, especially along the notoriously tortuous and winding Loch Lomondside road, it usually took him at least two and a half hours. A police driver showed at breakneck speed and with expert driving it could be done in two hours four minutes.

But the trump card for the police was what came to be known as 'the Ferrymaster's story'. The route which Mr. Watt was alleged to have taken to have committed the murders would have involved him crossing the Clyde on the Renfrew Ferry. In the early hours of the relevant day the Ferrymaster, Mr. John Taylor, said that around 3 a.m., a man drove his car on to the boat and was taken from the north side (the Lochgilphead end) to the south (the side the Watt house was on). He was not sure in the darkness of the make or colour of the car but he noted there were two occupants, the man and a large black dog sitting beside him. He gave a description which roughly fitted that of Mr. Watt (and countless other men). Photographs of Mr. Watt, his car and even his dog had been splashed on the front pages of every newspaper, it was the talk on everyone's lips and there were regular bulletins on the radio detailing the progress of the case. Mr. Taylor, an elderly man, knew all the details of the investigations long before he attended an identification parade and picked out Mr. Watt and long before he said the dog 'could' have been a black labrador.

The Crown Office decided to proceed and the distraught widower now faced the nightmare of being charged with the callous murders.

Things began to look up for the police when a Mr. Morrison suddenly decided it was his duty to step forward. He had been driving with his wife and two sons along the Loch Lomondside road around 2.30 a.m., on the relevant date when he saw a fast moving car approach along the lochside. He saw its headlights suddenly go out and wondered if it had landed in the loch but further on they came upon it parked off the road with no lights on. Thinking something might be wrong Mr. Morrison pulled up. There was a man in the car smoking with his hand half across his face. As Mr. Morrison got out, the car suddenly started up and sped off. He was not sure of the car's make and had seen no dog. Despite this fleeting glimpse in the dark Mr. Morrison managed to pick out Mr. Watt at an identification parade.

While all this was going on Manuel was languishing in Barlinnie, having been jailed for 18 months for the Hamilton Colliery canteen break-in. But all the talk and publicity centering on Mr. Watt was annoying him and he now decided it was about time he stole a bit of the limelight and if he could sicken the police at the same time so much the better. The fact that Mr. Watt and he were now both in the same prison added piquancy to the drama as far as he was concerned.

Manuel wrote to Mr. Watt's solicitor, Laurie Dowdall, saying he wanted to see him about his client and that it would be to their mutual advantage.

Mr. Dowdall later described what happened during the macabre interview, "He said Mr. Watt was innocent. So I said, "Well how do you know Mr. Watt is innocent? And his answer was, 'Because I know the man who did it'.

"So then I said to him, 'Well if you know the man who did it, why don't you go to the police?' He indicated in a few sentences that he regarded the police with some disapproval.

"I then said, 'Well, what was the name of the man?' and he didn't give me any name. So I said, 'Well, you had better tell me something about it'. He then told me that on the night before the Watts were murdered - and he made it clear that by the Watts he included Mrs. Brown - that a man had come to him and he had a gun in his possession, a revolver, and he wanted Mr. Manuel to go with him on a housebreaking expedition in Burnside.

"Mr. Manuel told me that he would not go with the man and that he did not go with him. He then said that he had read about the murders of these people in the paper and on the night that he had read about these murders the man came back to see him. This man he described as being in the horrors and he had a gun with him - the same gun. And he told Manuel that he had broken into the house at Fennsbank Avenue, number 18 I think he said, and then had gone down and broken into 5 Fennsbank Avenue and there he had shot three women. He wanted Manuel to get rid of the gun for him. Manuel said he took the gun from the man and the man also gave him a couple of rings. Now he described these rings to me and he said that each ring was an old fashioned type. One had had three stones, a diamond flanked by two rubies. The other he also described.

"I told Manuel that he might be pulling my leg. I asked him how I could be sure that he was telling me the truth. So he said, 'Well, I can give you information about the Watt house.' He then told me about the position of certain articles of furniture in the house and he described the position of the doors and in particular he described the door of what he called the girl's 'room. All this was something I would be able to check so I told him I would make some enquiries and come back. I left the establishment and telephoned Detective Superintendent Hendry who had charge of the investigation and told him I would like to see the interior of the Watt house. There I found that the description given by Manuel was an accurate one and I was quite satisfied that he had information which could be of interest to me in the defence of my client. So I went back to see him in the prison on a second occasion. I told him that I had verified the information but I said to him that I hadn't read or seen all the newspapers and you might have got this information from the press. So then he said, 'I can give you information on how the man got into the house'.

"According to Manuel the man entered by breaking the panel. He went into the bedroom on the left and shot the two women dead. One woman was shot twice in the head. He left that room and, as he left, the girl came out of another room. He struck her on the chin with his fist and knocked her out. He then tied the girl's hands behind her back and placed her on the bed. He left her there and then went round the house ransacking it and examining articles. On returning to the bedroom he saw the girl had come to, so he shot her through the head."

Mr. Dowdall left Barlinnie to check out this information and found out that one woman had indeed been shot twice so he went back for his third interview which he later described, "I asked him some more questions about the gun and I think it was at this meeting that he told me the man to whom he had referred had on some occasion prior to the Watt murders been in a house somewhere in the outskirts of Glasgow and he was there with a woman and it had been a housebreaking expedition and apparently there had been some kind of quarrel and the gun, which had been used in the Watt murders, had been fired and the bullet had gone into the bed.

"I then said to Manuel, 'Do you mean to tell me that the man who committed these horrible murders came to you and told you such unnecessary, piffling information as the disposition of articles of furniture in the house?' Manuel replied, 'Well, he did'. So I said, 'Well, that leads me to only one conclusion. I don't believe that and therefore you must know something more about this than you are telling me. Why don't you go to the police about it?' Again he indicated that he did not wish to go to the police and that he did not trust them.

"I said, 'Look Manuel, information such as you have and the suggestion that the man who committed these murders would start and tell you the piffling information about the furniture leads me to one conclusion - that you were there'. He said, 'Oh no, I wasn't there'. He insisted on this so that was the end of that conversation.

"At one of the meetings he sketched me a revolver and he told me that particular gun was a Webley Markiv."

Mr. Dowdall also received confidential information from another source. Another client and fellow prisoner told how Manuel had boasted that when the police searched his house after the Watt murders there had in fact been revolvers in a secret drawer.

And information reached the ears of the police from another source other than Manuel. An informer said a man named 'Scout' O'Neil had provided Manuel with a Webley revolver for a cash sum a week before the Watt murders. When interviewed about this O'Neil (his full name being James Tinney O'Neil) maintained the crooks unwritten code of silence and lyingly denied all knowledge of the deal.

A small army of police officers now descended on Manuel's house once more, to Manuel Senior's accusations of harassment, and went over it with a fine-tooth comb and once more found nothing.

Despite these frustrating setbacks the authorities finally realised they were holding the wrong man and on December 3rd Mr. Watt was allowed to walk free from Barlinnie. He had been in prison 67 days, an ordeal from which he never fully recovered. And even after Manuel was dead and gone the spiteful mutterings of the small minded claiming to be in the know continued to haunt him and up to his own death he was never completely free of the false gossip that he had something to do with the murders.

On November 30th 1957, Manuel was released from his eighteen months sentence and could not resist some more ghoulish pranks at the expense of Mr. Watt. He asked to meet him through Mr. Dowdall and the bizarre confrontation took place over many hours at the Whitehall Restaurant, at Jackson's Bar in Glasgow and at the home of Mr. Watt's brother. The sense of the absurd and the melodramatic once more tickled Manuel and he loved manipulating Mr. Watt as a dog plays with a bone it has chewed. At one of these meetings Manuel, being the centre of attention where he always wanted to be, named the murderer as one Charles Tallis and involved with him indirectly was a man called Martin Hart and Tallis's girlfriend, a woman named Mrs. Bowes. The tale Manuel spun was that Tallis, Hart and Mrs. Bowes had gone to 18 Fennsbank Avenue and broken in. They had afterwards gone along to identify the Valente house next door to the Watt house because Hart had told them that a large sum of money was in a safe there. But seeing Deanne Valente in the Watt house, as indeed she had been that night, they had mistaken the Watt house for the Valente house. In the early hours they returned, Tallis had broken the front panel of glass and they had gone in. The plan was to shoot everyone in the house except one who would be forced to disclose where the safe was and the key then the last one would also be shot.

Manuel again went into great detail about the things in the house. He told Mr. Watt that he had thrown Tallis's gun into the Clyde. He also told him the story about the bullet being fired into the bed of the house in Bothwell.

All of this reached the ears of the police but they had no concrete evidence on which to base a conviction since Manuel was bound to deny everything and say it was a frame-up and, besides, he was notorious as a liar, bluffer and boaster, always trying to be Mr. Big. (When the Burgess and McLean spy scandal broke Manuel claimed to have inside information and was actually flown to London by the police for questioning. He, in fact, knew nothing. But this was his style, always wanting to be centre stage in a big public drama. He could also put on a convincing American accent and say he was born in Manhattan, which was true, and that he had been a henchman of Al Capone, which was not.)

Within days of his last meeting with Mr. Watt, Manuel went off to Newcastle where he applied for a job on December 6th at the British Electrical Repairs factory in Shields Road where the transport manager later recalled the incident. The following day his movements are unknown but he was seen in the evening by a taxi driver in a cafe at the railway station. On December 8th he took a taxi at 4.30a.m., and headed for Edmondbyers, County Durham. The taxi driver was a bachelor named Sydney Dunn, aged 36. His mates at the station later identified Manuel because they recalled him ordering Mr. Dunn to take him to Edinburgh and they remembered remarking that Sydney had "knocked it off".

The following day Mr. Dunn's body was found 140 yards from his cab on the moors near Edmondbyers. Manuel had shot him in the back of the head and cut his throat because he had taken the wrong road. He had then in a fit of temper smashed all the windows and lights and left the cab looking like an abandoned wreck. On the 28th July the following year a Coroner's inquest found that Manuel had murdered Mr. Dunn.

The next incident occurred that same month on Christmas Day and it was back on home territory.

A house occupied by the Reverend Alexander Houston and his wife at 66 Wester Road, Mount Vernon, was broken into. The minister and his wife were fortunately visiting friends at the time. Entry had been made by breaking a panel in the kitchenette door. The front sitting room had been ransacked. Missing were a pair of sheepskin gloves, a Kodak camera and £2 in mixed coins. This break-in was to prove vital in the case against Manuel.

He gave the sheepskin gloves to his father and the camera to his sister Teresa as Christmas presents.

Three days later, midway between the Yuletide festivities and the New Year celebrations, the killer whose bloodlust was now rampant singled out 17-year-old pretty, dark haired, grey-eyed Isabelle Cooke as his next sacrificial victim. She lived with her parents and three younger brothers at 5 Carrick Drive, North Mount Vernon.

In the afternoon the parents left the house and did not return until eight in the evening by which time Isabelle had left to go to a dance at Uddingston. The parents went to bed but lay awake listening for Isabelle to return. When she had not done so by 12.30a.m., this was so out of character that Mr. Cooke got out of bed, got dressed and with a torch went out to look for her. Fifty yards from the house was a path by a works railway, an unlit short cut which led to Mount Vernon Avenue and the bus stop. He knew his daughter was in the habit of taking this path, the same one on which, eleven years previously, Mrs. K. had been attacked.

Mr. Cooke flashed his torch around in the darkness but saw nothing and eventually returned home. Their telephone was out of order and they assumed Isabelle must have decided to spend the night with a girl friend but had been unable to let them know.

However, by ten in the morning with still no word they went to the police. At teatime a constable called at their house and showed the distraught parents a small cosmetic bag which had been found: it was Isabelle's. Later they returned with other articles which had been found on waste ground, all belonging to the missing girl: a vanity case, a short raincoat, a fan and a spray of imitation flowers.

A murder squad was formed under the charge of Detective Inspector John Rae. (Supt. Hendry had coincidentally retired on the very day of Isabelle's disappearance.)

It had been a cold, pitch black night and she had been supposed to meet her boyfriend at a bus stop in Uddingston. When she had failed to turn up he had gone on to the dance alone, assuming she had done the same.

In the case of Isabelle - as in that of Anne Knielands - someone had heard a cry in the night. A woman and her dog had been in their back garden which was beside the unlit path Isabelle had to walk along. Suddenly, somewhere in the darkness, a feminine voice cried out in fear. The dog heard it too and began to bark. But the woman, straining her ears into the night wind, heard nothing further and took no action.

A full scale search of the area was launched and some of her clothing was found in the River Calder while a handbag was found in a disused colliery air shaft.

It was while Supt. Muncie was searching round the shaft that the county's Chief Constable John Wilson appeared to inform him that three people had been found shot dead in their bungalow in Uddingston. The date was January 6th 1958 and the family had been dead for six days.

They were forty-five-year old Peter Smart, his wife Doris and their 11-year-old son Michael. They had been shot in the head as they lay in their beds in the early hours of New Year's Day while parties had been going on in bungalows all around them. (Manuel must have entered their home sometime after 6a.m. because he was at his parents house celebrating New Year up till then; but having committed the murders he also spent around four hours in the house admiring his handiwork and relaxing in the comfort of the luxury bungalow as if this in itself was a symbolic form of rape and defiance combined.)

Four nights after this a Mr. and Mrs. McMunn were asleep in their home near the Smarts when they awoke with a start. Something had disturbed them and when Mr. McMunn switched on the light and saw a man's face at the bedroom door he shouted to his startled wife, "Where's the gun?" (There was no gun; he was wisely bluffing.) The man then ran off down the stairs, out of the house and away. The McMunns were lucky. Manuel had by this time flung his tell-tale gun into the Clyde off the King George V bridge.

Detectives investigating the Smart murders found that the dead civil engineer's Austin 35 had been found abandoned in Florence Street, Gorbals, but enquiries in that area did not turn up anything.

Lanarkshire was now living in a state of fear verging on panic. All the paraphernalia of security-locks of every description, alarm bells, peep holes, bolts, door chains and guard dogs were in terrific demand and neighbours made pacts to keep their eyes open and make regular telephone calls to each other.

A few hours after he had committed the Smart murders Manuel had gone to his old pal Joe Brannan's house and said he had a lot of money. Asked where he got it, he replied that he had gone into Glasgow and collected £30 and more at the

Gordon Club in connection with the Watt murders. He said there had been some difficulty but he had got the money in the end. But it was money spent by Manuel which was his undoing.

After the Smart murders it was belatedly decided to call in the help of Glasgow C.I.D., and Detective Superintendent Alex Brown and Detective Inspector Tom Goodall joined the hunt. It was decided to enlist the help of a member of the underworld and the obvious choice was Joe Brannan, Manuel's true and trusted friend, the one who had refused to name him as the accomplice all those years ago, the one Manuel went to after the Smart murders. Detective Inspector Robert McNeill was the one selected to approach Joe, a villain who like other notable underworld figures, was horrified at what was going on, not simply out of decent basic human feelings but also because the heat was on every man with a record as the combined police forces of central Scotland got more desperate to catch the killer.

Manuel's style upset the Glasgow underworld. Where he wanted to be flamboyant and in the limelight they preferred the anonymous shadows, committing crimes without getting their names known at all. For Manuel being well-known was a vital part of the game.

For these reasons it had been decided among Glasgow's criminal fraternity that Manuel had to go and, therefore, Joe Brannan agreed to help trap him and began to hang around with him, buying plenty of drink courtesy of police funds. It was unofficial liaison between the jacks and knaves which helped close the case. Every night around midnight Joe met a police officer and reported to him on the evening's conversation and what Manuel had let slip.

From Joe they learned where Manuel had spent his New Year's Day money and they checked the specified pubs to see if the money tallied with the new notes Mr. Smart had obtained from the bank. These were Commercial Bank of Scotland notes and some of them were still traceable, although there were only hours before they would have been in circulation among customers. The money Manuel had spent in the first fortnight of January matched with money taken from the Smart house. The net was beginning to close and the murder squad decided to swoop on Manuel's house once more. They arrived at 6.45 in the morning and removed his clothing for forensic examination to the usual remonstrations about harassment from his father. They found nothing to connect with the Smart murders in the house but they did find a pair of sheepskin gloves and a Kodak camera which were the property of the Reverend Houston. Teresa told how the camera was a Christmas gift from Peter. And Sam, the father, told how the gloves were also a gift from his thoughtful son.

Sam was taken to Bellshill Police Station and locked up, the charge being possession of stolen property. He was then further charged with breaking into the Houston house along with his son Peter.

At Hamilton Police Headquarters the following day Manuel was put on an identification parade for the money he had passed in pubs and hotels and numerous people picked him out. Manuel then asked to see Supt. Brown and told him that the notes he had in his possession had been given him by Samuel 'Dandy' McKay of the Gordon Club. Manuel claimed he had met 'Dandy' between 10 and 10.30 on the morning of New Year's Day which was an unfortunate time to choose because a local shopkeeper in Uddingston had seen Manuel near his home at that time. Manuel claimed he had met 'Dandy' near the Airport Bus terminal in St. Enoch's Square in Glasgow and said he had sat in 'Dandy's' car and received from him £50, of which 30 were in £5 notes and 20 in blue £1 notes. The money had allegedly been paid for showing 'Dandy' around the Sheepburn Road area where he was supposed to be going to break into a bookmaker's house.

But Manuel could not have chosen a worse figure than 'Dandy' to implicate because he was a popular, flamboyant, gregarious character with a reputation as a clean type of villain. The idea that he would break into a house and kill in cold blood was out of the question and detectives knew this. In response to a police request 'Dandy' called at Hamilton Police Station, the H.Q. of Manuel's much hated Lanarkshire force, on the evening of January 14th and was deliberately confronted with Manuel who told him nervously. "Sammy, I'm sorry I had to tell them about the money you gave me."

'Dandy' made a move to approach Manuel but was gently restrained. He glared at the killer and snapped, "You've made the biggest mistake of your life - you're going to swing!"

Manuel, white faced and visibly shaken, was led away.

In the eyes of his friends in the criminal fraternity where he wielded a great deal of influence 'Dandy' was and always had been completely trustworthy when it came to his fellow villains but now he felt no loyalty towards a creature who would shoot innocent defenceless people, especially children, in their beds and then try to frame him for such diabolical crimes. This infuriated him and he decided to help the police put Manuel out of the way forever. He told senior detectives that he knew Manuel was in possession of a Beretta on December 19th. He had given Manuel a lift to a house in Florence Street (where Mr. Smart's car had later been found abandoned) where a brown paper parcel was to be collected. This turned out to be a gun which Manuel showed off to 'Dandy' who had no idea the horrible use to which it was to be put. He had been told it was only for self protection. 'Dandy' continued to elaborate on all he knew about Manuel, which was quite a lot, and the detectives listened with growing interest.

That same evening an identification parade was held and Mrs. McMunn picked out Manuel as the man who had peered in at the bedroom door and 'Dandy' also officially picked out Manuel as the possessor of the Beretta.

At 11.10 that night the police charged Manuel with the Smart murders as well as breaking into the minister's house and the McMunn's house.

The following day Manuel asked to speak to Inspector McNeil but the detective kept the killer waiting several hours to keep his nerves frayed before, along with Inspector Goodall, he went to see him. Manuel said he wanted to clear up certain unsolved crimes in the area but before he would say any more he wanted to see his mother and father. At this point he said, "Bring my mother and father here and I will speak to them with you present and once I have told them myself and made a clean breast of it you can take them away and I will clear up everything for you and I will take you to where the girl Cooke is buried."

He was asked if he wanted a solicitor but replied, "I want to do this myself. I will write something out for you."

He was given paper and wrote, addressing it to Inspector McNeil:

I hereby promise you personally that I am prepared to give information to you that will enable you to clear up a number of unknown crimes which occurred in the County of Lanark in the past two years. This promise is given that I might release my father and my family from any obligation or loyalties they may feel on my behalf. I wish to see my parents and make a clean breast with them first. The crimes I refer to are crimes o,f homicide. I further wish to stress that I volunteer this statement of my own free will without duress or pressure of any description being brought to bear on me

On reading over this statement he did not seem too happy about it so he wrote a second one couched in roughly the same terms but with the added sentence, *"I will lead information about the following specific crimes: 1) Anne Knielands 2) the Watt murders 3) Isabelle Cooke 4) the Smart murders."*

Inspector McNeil said he would have to consult with the Procurator Fiscal to see if he could be allowed to see his parents and at this Manuel blurted out, almost desperately, that he wanted to tell them about the Smart murders. He said he entered the house around 6a.m., on New Year's Day. He said he shot the man and then the woman and then the boy, although he said he thought the boy was in fact a man. He then stole some money, took the car keys and drove the car eventually to Florence Street where he left it. He threw the gun in the Clyde and the car keys in the Calder.

His parents were brought to see him and tearfully he told them, "There's no future for me. I have done some terrible things. I killed the girl Knielands at East Kilbride and I shot the three women in the house at Burnside."

Later that evening he was taken to Barlinnie to comply with the commital warrant. Although it was nearly midnight another warrant was obtained almost immediately to take him out again to show the police where Isabelle Cooke was buried.

It was a pitch black, bitterly cold night. He directed a cavalcade of police and press cars to a lonely field near Baillieston Brickworks where arc lights were quickly set up and shovels unloaded from vans. Handcuffed to two detectives Manuel walked up and down the field trying to get his bearings in the dark. He remarked that the field had been ploughed since the last time he had been there. Suddenly he stopped, looked around him and said, "I think she is in there." And he tapped his shoe on the dirt, "I think I am standing on her."

Her shoes were found first then the police unearthed her rigid, decomposing, semi-naked body.

A few days later by an extraordinary coincidence Mr. James Platt, whose house in Douglas Drive had been broken into the night before the Watt murders, walked into his local police station with a bullet which had been fired into his mattress. His wife who had been thinking of getting a new bed and had been examining the old one had just found it. The bullet was rushed to the police ballistics department and it was found to have been fired by the Watt murder weapon. Detectives then went back to Manuel's house and found an electric shaver which had been stolen from the Platt house.

Manuel's trial began at Glasgow High Court on Monday 12th May 1958. The judge was Lord Cameron (who had defended Patrick Carraher on his first murder charge) and the jury was made up of nine men and six women. The trial lasted sixteen days. The prosecution was led by Mr. M. G. Gillies assisted by Mr. Ronald Sutherland who had to take over after three days when Mr. Gillies was taken ill. The defence was conducted by Mr. H. Leslie Q.C.

The indictment charged Manuel with all eight murders. (The taxi driver's murder could not be tried in Scotland and was left in abeyance for the moment.) Manuel put forward special defences: to some a simple 'not guilty'. To the Smart murders he put forward alibi, to the murder of the Watts he put forward impeachment and to both break-ins in Fennsbank Avenue he put forward the same defence. His impeachment in the murder charge was of Mr. Watt based on the Ferryman's story and the fact that the police had charged him; on the break-ins he blamed Charles Tallis and Mrs. Mary Bowes, the people he had claimed were responsible during his unusual conversations with Mr. Watt.

As regards his confessions to the police made at Hamilton Police Headquarters he now claimed they had been extorted by threats involving his parents. The evidence against him was formidable but he put up a strong rearguard action. He was now in his beloved position - the centre of attraction. The media throughout the world were full of him. Queues waited for hours outside the court to get a seat. It was, as they say, the biggest show in town. His name was on everybody's lips. This was his hour.

But as the trial progressed even this was not enough for him. He seemed to be a passive observer in the drama and not an active participant so he decided to take the stage himself. On the ninth day he dismissed his counsel and, like all those years ago at Airdrie Sheriff Court, undertook his own defence.

This time he was not to be so successful but, nevertheless, Lord Cameron complimented him on his quick brain and eloquence.

When Mr. Watt came to give evidence he had to be carried in on a stretcher and it was a grim sight to see, surrounded by all the hushed panoply of the Law, the wrecked shell of a man being baited, taunted and accused of his family's murder by the man who had committed the deed. It appealed to Manuel's sadistic sense of humour. Mr. Watt struggled to bear up under the onslaught and stoutly, repeatedly, denied all the innuendos and falsifications which Manuel flung at him. It was an added essence of torture for this most unfortunate of men.

As the trial neared its inevitable conclusion Manuel's self confidence began to waver. His hands shook, his face took on a yellowish pallor and he sweated a great deal. Gone was the old swagger and braggadocio. It was replaced with a dark, sullen moody stare.

The jury had no doubt about their verdict - guilty on all charges except the Knielands murder where there was not enough evidence to convict. Lord Cameron duly put on the black cap and sentenced Manuel to "death by hanging."

He appealed, again on the grounds that the confessions had been due to police pressure via his father (against whom all charges had been dropped once Manuel had confessed) but it was a hopeless gesture. The appeal was turned down. Deciding now to clear the records once and for all, and in the process doing an about turn that was an insulting gesture to the Appeal Court judges, he confessed to three more murders - that of Helen Carlin, a prostitute who was known as 'Red Helen' who had been strangled in Pimlico in September 1954 (preceding the first Lanarkshire murder, perhaps it too was a rehearsal); that of Anne Steele, a 55-year-old spinster found battered to death in Glasgow on January 11th 1956 (nine days after the Knielands murder); and that of Ellen Petrie, known as 'English Nellie', who was stabbed in Glasgow in June 1956 (midway between the Knielands and Watt murders). In all then, Manuel's known murder victims totalled a round dozen but there could have been others which for his own unfathomable reasons he did not want to reveal.

There were three motives behind Manuel's killings. The first was revenge against the Lanarkshire Police force who he believed had ruined his life because of wrongful imprisonment for rape and he sought to humiliate and tantalise with a spate of unsolved, lurid murders in a small area of their patch.

The second motive was sexual. Manuel was impotent and could only get sexual gratification through masturbation, the humiliation of women or the sense of fulfilment pulling the trigger of a gun gave him. In the Airdrie case where Manuel had earlier on in his criminal career successfully defended himself on an indecent assault charge, the victim had testified that her attacker had dragged her into a field and threatened her with a knife. He forced her to remove her underwear. Revelling in her terror, his threats of violence had become more and more extreme as his excitement mounted. Then he had suddenly calmed down and allowed the woman to leave unmolested. Later when. he was arrested, Manuel's trousers were found to be stained with semen. The terror of his victim, coupled with her humiliation and the baring of her private parts, had aroused him to such an extent that there was ejaculation and no further action was necessary.

Similarly, with the murders there was humiliation but no sexual molestation or rape. Anne Knielands had her knickers ripped off, a nylon was stolen and her dress was up round her waist when she was found. Isabelle Cooke was semi-naked when exhumed and her panties and underslip were never recovered. In the Watt killings Mrs. Brown's green pyjama trousers had been ripped from the waistband down the right leg. Vivienne's pyjama trousers had been removed altogether, the buttons of her yellow and black pyjama top were strewn about the room, her pink brassiere which she had been wearing was torn off and there were semen stains on the cover of her bed. In the Smart killings, Mrs. Doris Smart's nightdress was ripped and she was found nakedly exposed. For Manuel the degradation of his victims was enough.

The third motive for the murders was simply that Manuel wanted to be famous. His egomania was a burning lust inside him which would not rest until he saw himself emblazoned across the front pages. This phenomena was fairly new and incomprehensible in Manuel's day but from Lee Harvey Oswald onward there have been plenty of small men wanting to go down in history for a seemingly senseless criminal act.

Allied to his egomania went Manuel's arrogance, his contempt for the law and belief that he was too clever to be caught, his certainty in his own ability to get away with it. This led him to take hair raising or, to him, thrilling risks. When he took the Smarts' car after their murder he gave a lift to a policeman who happened to be going on duty to help look for Isabelle Cooke's body. Manuel laughed and chatted with the policeman and dropped him off with the parting comment, "I think they're looking in the wrong place!"

During his time in the death cell Manuel clammed up and never spoke to any of the prison officers. He put on two stones in weight and never showed any sign of remorse. His one comment on his terrible crimes showed how callous his feelings were, even on the threshold of eternity. As he was given exercise in the prison yard between two burly prison officers he said to a prisoner he knew, the only other one taking exercise at the time, "What do you think of that bastard McKay?" referring to 'Dandy' breaking the underworld code and giving information to Manuel's arch enemies - the police. He was more annoyed at this than he was about the blood on his hands.

He spent a quiet night before his death and on the morning of Friday July 11th 1958 he literally ran onto the scaffold inside the walls of Barlinnie Prison where the trap door dropped at one minute past eight. He could not get it over quickly enough. The reign of terror was over. The mad wolf was dead.

Chapter four:
THE MAN IN THE WOOD

Around 1.45a.m., in the early morning darkness of Sunday 23rd July, 1961 in the middle of Glasgow's annual Fair holiday a taxi pulled up outside a house in the Castlemilk housing estate on the city's southern outskirts. The voices of two men were heard talking by people in the nearest houses. The motor was still running and the taxi radio's crackling could be faintly heard. Then there were two loud bangs. The curious who went to their windows saw under the streetlights a man running towards the darkness of a nearby wood. Doors opened, people became curious and glanced into the cab. The driver lay slouched over his wheel, dripping with blood and the windscreen was shattered. One of the shocked residents used the car radio to summon help while others dialled 999. Within minutes the street was packed with other taxis and police cars. But it was too late. The driver was dying from two gun-shot wounds and his murderer had got clean away. The crime was apparently motiveless and for many the ghastly fear arose that a second Manuel had arisen to emulate the horrors of the first.

Three months later the man accused of this capital crime stood in the dock, a slightly built, medium sized, thirty-year-old criminal with a particularly pallid skin which served to accentuate his dark, slicked back hair and coal black eyes. Immaculately dressed with strong regular features, he appeared to many to be a cocky young prince of evil faintly reminiscent of Manuel. There was certainly something chilling and throughout the years he became known as one of Glasgow's most dangerous criminals. His name was Walter Scott Ellis.

The man he was accused of murdering was a mild mannered, hard work-ing husband and father who had spent years building up his taxi fleet of five cabs. His name was John Walkinshaw.

Within seconds of the trial being over, it was obvious who was to be the feted hero of the hour splashed before the public's gaze in an unseemly scramble by newspapers to glorify the undeserving.

But at first things looked black for Ellis, not least because no lawyer want-ed anything to do with his case. Partly this was because the Ellis family had little money (this was in the days before legal aid), but there was also strong public feel-ing against anyone trying to protect the accused in such a heinous crime.

However, at the end of the day this worked out to Ellis's advantage because he ended up with a young, up and coming lawyer who was ready to work 25 hours a day to make a name for himself. His name was Joseph Beltrami and he was the same age as Ellis. This trial was to make both their reputations although their paths were to go in diametrically opposite directions.

Before the trial began at Glasgow High Court, Beltrami had interviewed each of the 125 witnesses on the prosecution list at least twice. In addition he had visited the places involved dozens of times as well as studying forensic aspects involved in the case.

He chose to help a young advocate also keen to make a name for himself,

Nicholas Fairbairn, who was later to become a Tory M.P. in Sir Alec Douglas Home's old seat, as well as Solicitor General for Scotland. This was the first big case that Beltrami and Fairbairn had worked on and they were to be a formidable team for several years, the first hardworking, rather dour but sharp as a scalpel, the second flamboyant with a touch of the actor about him. They both had that flair for publicity which is vital for all successful criminal lawyers - Beltrami even organised his own press conferences after trials and became as big a personality as anybody else involved in a case in the true Clarence Darrow tradition.

Beltrami also instructed a senior counsel, Ronald Bennet Q.C., to help Fairbairn because the defence was complex and the Judge, seventy-two-year-old Lord Patrick, approved the unique motion before the trial began that the defence would be split with Fairbairn cross examining on technical aspects of the evidence and Bennet covering the straightforward factual questions as well as summing up.

Advocate Depute Norman Wylie was the formidable head of the prosecution team. He too was later to become a Tory M.P. as well as a Lord Advocate and Senator of the College of Justice.

The murder had taken place in Tormusk Road next to Glen Wood. There had been no eyewitnesses to tie the accused in with the pulling of the trigger. For both sides the case was to revolve round purely circumstantial evidence as well as timing and distances which was to be expected with a taxi driver as the victim.

The trial began inauspiciously for Ellis. Beltrami and his two helpers decided to withdraw a Special Defence of Alibi. This was because they felt their client would not cut a very credible figure under cross-examination. He could be argumentative and aggressive and it was felt the jury should not see this side of his character but merely the neat, mute young man sitting unmoved before them. Besides Mr. Wylie was good at getting even the most credible defence witnesses tongue-tied. All that the defence could now do was discredit the prosecution evidence and rely on that alone.

After the black dressed widow had given evidence about having to identify her husband's body in hospital in the early hours of the morning (evidence unlikely to help the accused in the subjective minds of the jury), a map was produced in court and various taxi routes discussed.

The two most important streets involved were Mill Street, Bridgeton, on the south side of the city, where Ellis had been in a taxi shortly before the murder and Ardencraig Road on the other side of Glen Wood from the scene of the murder. Mill Street was almost four miles away from the scene of the murder and Ardencraig Road about a quarter of a mile.

Next witnesses were people at a party near the murder scene who told of phoning for a taxi, seeing Walkinshaw's and hearing the shots. Two witnesses told of seeing a man wearing a light suit running towards the wood carrying something white in his right hand which could have been a handkerchief. The defence made something of the light coloured suit since Ellis had been wearing a dark coloured one on the night of the murder but what the prosecution had failed to discover (possibly by not visiting the scene of the crime at night as Beltrami had done numerous times) was that the street lighting was of the orange sodium variety and liable to play tricks with light and shade.

What was agreed was that whoever ran for the wood knew the area because he made straight for a hidden stone bridge over a burn. It was also generally agreed that this man who vanished into the pitch darkness of the trees must have been the gunman.

It was also established that 10/4d was on Walkinshaw's meter when his body was found and that he radioed in and said he was dropping a fare at Tormusk Road shortly before he died there and that he was travelling from the south, the direction of Mill Street.

The most damning prosecution evidence came from another taxi driver who pointed to Ellis in the dock and said he was the man he had picked up in Ardencraig Road beside Glen Wood around 15 minutes after the murder, in other words the same time it would have taken the killer to run through the wood after the murder and turn up on the other side in time to hail another cab and get out of the area. Ellis had also been carrying a handkerchief in his right hand according to this taxi driver. The trip was only three quarters of a mile to where Elis's parents stayed and the fare was only two shillings, despite which the passenger gave the driver five.

The defence could do little with this witness. He had picked out Ellis at an identification parade and was unshakeable in his conviction that he had been the passenger. He even mentioned the dark suit. All the defence could establish was that the passenger seemed composed and reasonably talkative with nothing at all to indicate he had just ran through a lengthy wood in pitch darkness after a murder. In private the defence could not resolve this impasse with their client. He simply denied knowing anything about it and said the driver must be mistaken.

Things were not looking too good for Ellis at this stage but at least the next witness, a fingerprint expert, said he had found no prints of any value in Walkinshaw's taxi.

Police witnesses next told how they had saturated the area and among the people interviewed was Ellis who lied that he had spent Saturday night and Sunday morning at his parents house. In fact, he had been at a party in Mill Street until around 1.15a.m., when he left in a taxi. There were plenty of witnesses who came forward to verify this, except one - the taxi driver who had picked him up. Despite newspaper appeals and personal written appeals to Glasgow's 1,280 registered taxi drivers not one came forward to say he had picked up Ellis outside the party in Mill Street. The inference was obvious.

When Ellis was arrested he insisted he had been indoors with his parents at all the relevant times. Next, detectives told of a visit they made to a flat Ellis recently bought on the south side. In a matchbox there they found eleven live cartridges but no gun.

However, returns in taxis from Mill Street to the scene of the crime threw up discrepancies. If Ellis had got into Walkinshaw's taxi at 1.15a.m., from the party it would only have taken him ten minutes to get to the scene of the murder which took place around 1.45a.m., and the fare would only have been 8/ - and not 10/4d. But only the dead man could tell the times and places he had travelled through before his death.

What the police did discover by jogging through Glen Wood was that the man picked up in Ardencraig Road could have been the killer. What they failed to do was make plaster casts of prints in the wood immediately after the shooting and possibly crucial evidence was washed away with overnight rain.

Other witnesses told how when he got the taxi from the party in Mill Street Ellis had said he was going to his parents house in Castlemilk. The prosecution case was that after committing the murder Ellis had ran through the wood, picked up another taxi and made the short trip to his parents, and yes, neighbours of the Ellises had heard someone enter the close at the time in question but, no, they had no idea who it was.

Witnesses at the party said Ellis had been drinking heavily and when he left he had been carrying a small brown parcel and seemed very solicitous over it.

Police forensic evidence showed that green and clear glass fragments found in one of Ellis's shoes could have come from the scene of the crime where glass from the shattered windscreen and a broken beer bottle lay on the pavement.

Lengthy, often boring and technical questioning from Fairbairn on this point managed to take much of the sting out of this part of the prosecution's case. He established that the glass involved, both at the murder scene and on Ellis's shoe, was so common as to make a similarity almost meaningless.

Another plus of sorts for the defence was the establishment that the bullets in Ellis's possession were not of the same kind which killed Walkinshaw. What could not be denied was that Ellis should never have had the bullets in the first place and the reason for their possession was never touched upon. Extensive searches by the police had also failed to uncover the whereabouts of the pocket pistol in the case which could have fired either type of bullet.

The Prosecution closed their case after three days of circumstantial but nevertheless powerful evidence.

The Defence began by calling a man who had been wrongly picked out at an identification parade, in which Ellis took part, by two witnesses who saw the runner to the wood. But they had only said the man was of the general build and appearance and anyway the man had been racing off with his back to them.

The Defence also established that the windscreen glass on the pavement could have fallen there after the killer had run off. A witness said he had also been drinking in a pub with Ellis shortly before his arrest and that the floor had showed remnants of recently dropped beer glasses.

When it came time for his summing up, Mr. Wylie put the Prosecution's case forcibly. He pointed out to the jury, "My case consists of circumstantial evidence but such evidence is a perfectly valid way of establishing a criminal offence". The Prosecution maintained Ellis had got into Walkinshaw's taxi in Mill Street with the object of going to the Ellis household in Castlemilk, that Ellis had shot the driver then sprinted through Glen Wood to Ardencraig Road where the other driver drove him to his parents home. Mr. Wylie stressed the unshakeable identification made by the second driver and went on, "Is it not strange that Ellis should have required two taxis to take him home? My submission is that the reason he changed taxis is perfectly obvious - because he shot the driver who took him in the first place to Tormusk Road. We have a murderer running into a wood - and a quarter of an hour later you find the accused Ellis, standing at the opposite end of the wood looking for a taxi."

Mr. Wylie sat down after an hour and it was then the turn of the Defence. Beltrami, Fairbairn and Bennet had gone over this speech for hour upon hour as if they were preparing an oscar winning scenario and when Mr. Bennet stood up to deliver it the result was quite masterly. It had to be.

The first point made was that a guilty verdict would mean the accused swinging at the end of a rope. The onus of proof was on the Crown and they had to prove guilt "beyond reasonable doubt".

Mr Bennet stressed the lack of fingerprints, the lack of a weapon and the fact that the bullets in Ellis's possession did not match those which had killed Walkinshaw. He pointed out Ellis had not been picked out at an identity parade by the people who saw the man running into the wood, that Ellis had been drinking heavily that night and was in no state to run anywhere.

When it came to the evidence of the second taxi driver who had picked up the man in Ardencraig Road, Mr. Bennet said that if it had been Ellis he was wearing a dark coloured suit whereas one witness had said the man who had run into the wood was wearing a light coloured suit (ignoring the effect of the street lights which the Defence knew all about) and that the man, whoever he was, showed no indication whatsoever of having run through a thick wood in pitch darkness. And Mr. Bennet posed the question, "Would a killer attract attention to himself by hailing another taxi for a distance of only a few hundred yards and in the near vicinity of his crime?"

With regards to the glass particles, Mr. Bennet dismissed them thus, "There has been evidence, which is not in dispute that most clear glass is made by one firm - Pilkington's. That being so, little can be drawn from the fact that the clear glass found in the heel was of a similar density to the same type of glass found at the scene of the crime. Equally, the green beer-bottle glass was manufactured by the Scottish Central Glassworks of Alloa, who are the main suppliers to a number of breweries. These bottles are very common indeed, and the density of them cannot really vary to any marked extent."

The discrepancies in distances and fares between Mill Street and Castlemilk, between the reality of such a journey and the thesis as put forward by the Prosecution, were pointed out.

Mr. Bennet ended, "It is not sufficient for you to say that he might have done it. Before convicting you would require to be satisfied beyond reasonable doubt that he had done it."

Lord Patrick who now began his summing up was renowned for his impartiality and his address to the jury lived up to this reputation to an almost punctilious degree.

He told them, "The proof in the case, if there was proof, would depend wholly on circumstantial evidence. People sneer at that but these are uninformed people who do not understand that it is every bit as reliable as other evidence. Very often there are no eyewitnesses to a crime, and everything depends on circumstantial evidence."

Referring to the seriousness of the crime involved, he went on, "If the accused is found guilty he will be hanged by the neck. But that is not a concern of yours or mine." Some of the jury winced slightly at this. "You are here to hear the evidence and make up your minds on that."

Then he brought up one of the main arguments for the Defence, "It is important that you, the jury, should pay attention to the question of the burden of proof. You must be satisfied beyond reasonable doubt of the accused's guilt before you would be justified in bringing in a guilty verdict. It is not necessary to prove motivation. It is quite true, as both Crown and Defence have indicated, that the time factor is important. The theory of the Crown is that Ellis got in Walkinshaw's taxi in Mill Street and travelled to the scene of the crime where he shot Walkinshaw and then, in another street nearby, hired another taxi."

Referring to the fact that Ellis had lied to the police that he had been with his parents when he had been out at a party, Lord Patrick said, "Even if you hold that Ellis told lies to the police, that does not prove that he was there at the scene of the crime and committed it. There could be a number of reasons for Ellis's lying to the police unconnected with involvement in this crime."

Remarking on the evidence of the glass found on Ellis's shoes, he pointed out that the Crown's point was the remarkable coincidence of the two types of glass being there - both clear and green - as there was alleged to have been beside Walkinshaw's taxi.

Finally Lord Patrick instructed the jury on the three verdicts they could return - guilty, not guilty and not proven. Those who had been actively campaigning for the abolition of capital punishment and who had shown an interest in this case wondered later if, at this stage, the punishment in prospect had been life imprisonment instead of hanging there might not have been a completely different attitude on the part of the jury.

When the jury retired it was thought that following a complicated trial they would be out for some time. To everyone's surprise the jury bell rang after only half an hour. Ellis rose and in the total silence the foreman of the jury gave their verdict "Not proven - unanimously!"

Ellis, grinning with relief, shook the hands of his counsel while taxi drivers in the public gallery, who had organised an appeal fund for their dead colleague's widow, muttered about the deficiencies in the jury system.

The crowd of around three hundred gathered around the court steps were then treated to the unappetising spectacle of the city's press literally fighting to get their hands on Ellis for his exclusive story. A mass of tumbling fighting bodies fell down the court steps as blows were freely exchanged. One large photographer, before charging into the melee, took out his false teeth and placed them in his hip pocket for safety. He was promptly kicked in the behind and they were broken, much to his pain and anger. Ellis was eventually bundled by one daily newspaperman into what he thought was his paper's car. It in fact belonged to the opposition and sped off with Ellis in the back seat, leaving the reporter stranded and panic stricken. Beltrami was there on the court steps to start a lifelong love affair with the press and a less amicable one with the police who converged on the scene to restore order. Editors were later summoned before the Chief Constable to give a guarantee that such unseemly behaviour would not be repeated.

Ellis, smoking a cigar and jubilantly celebrating, was pictured on the front page of one newspaper. He had sold his story for a hundred pounds and was quoted as saying, "I think John Walkinshaw was shot by a roving madman lurking in the

Castlemilk woods - by a man who may strike again. I had nothing at all to do with this ghastly, pointless murder."

It was to be the high point of Ellis's criminal career. Always keen on armed robbery, boastful that he had cheated the gallows and could flaunt the law, he eventually was too casual and was cornered trying to hold up a bank in Pollokshaws in 1966.

Sentencing him to a punitive 21 years for attempted murder and armed robbery, the judge said that while he was at large the lives of innocent members of the public were at risk.

At first, Ellis served his time quietly, saying to his cellmates that he wanted full remission so that when he got out he could shoot as many policemen as soon as possible. Then he started smuggling out letters to the press complaining that he, a model prisoner, was being treated harshly while others who had caused trouble inside had been moved to a life of comparative luxury in Barlinnie's Special Unit. He also complained to everybody who would listen that he had not been given any form of training or help to face the outside world on his release and that he feared drifting back to his old criminal ways and ending up back in prison.

His fears proved prophetic because a few months after his release (after serving 14 years) he made a bungled attempt at holding up a licensed grocer's shop, using a toy replica gun. Unfortunately for him the two shopkeepers behind the counter, 21-year-old Jack Mohammed and his 19-year-old brother Teddy, were karate enthusiasts willing to 'have a go'. Ellis, who was masked, shouted, "Okay sambo - hold them up!"

At first, the surprised brothers thought it was a sick joke then Ellis fired a blank and pistol whipped Jack. Teddy promptly grabbed a cheese knife, closed his eyes and ran at the robber. After a struggle and a 100-yard sprint along the street, Ellis was ignominiously disarmed and incapacitated by a few well chosen blows. The fact that he was drunk helped the brothers.

His appearance in court was pathetic and his snivelling, grovelling plea in mitigation, which he performed himself this time, was quite a come-down for the once arrogant gangster. In tears he said he had been "tossed out" of prison with no attempt having been made to rehabilitate him. He had no job, had been staying at a hostel and he told the Sherrif, "I was besotted by drink and, as often happens on these occasions, I had every intention of going straight but was tempted by the devil." He was sentenced to three years imprisonment. It was a long way from champagne and cigars.

Chapter five:
THE PHOENIX

In the sixties the Press correctly labelled James 'Babyface' Boyle as Scotland's most dangerous criminal and Glasgow's worst gangster following the eclipse of Walter Scott Ellis. But there was more to Boyle than that grim accolade. Not only was he unique in being acquitted on two separate murder charges before being 'sent down' on a third, but from sculpting human flesh with his bayonet he took to sculpting clay, having his exhibits displayed at the Edinburgh Festival, and from being the ringleader of one of the country's worst prison riots he ended up being at the centre of a controversy over a Special Unit which it is now recognised leads the field in prison reform.

His remarkable career in crime began in the Gorbals where he was born in a tenement slum in the spring of 1944, the third of a family of four. His father was a streetfighter and member of the notorious Bee Hive Gang and although he died, partly because of wounds sustained over the years, when Boyle was young he was still talked about admiringly by local hoodlums long after his untimely demise and there was thus a violent reputation for young Boyle to live up to.

In the slum district's sub-culture men who were handy with their fists, as well as being rebels and outlaws generally, were admired. Many of the poverty stricken families who had to share in many cases single-ends (one roomed flats) or rooms and kitchens with their usually numerous children owed little or no allegiance to the Establishment or its representatives whether it be the rent collector, the clerk who handed out the dole money, the gaffer if you were employed, the education authorities or the police. And men who made their drab lives more adventurous or gave the 'V' sign to the authorities were often openly talked of as if they were local heroes. Brawlers and villains like Boyle's father or the venerated Dan Cronin, whose funeral was attended by more mourners than any Lord Provost's, were princes in their own society, people apart to be copied and Boyle, who felt himself to be a cut above the rest of his pals because of his bloodstock, saw nothing to stop him emulating his father's deeds and there were many who actively encouraged him.

Allied to their fighting abilities (and who is to say there is that much difference between a legal boxing match and an illegal bout in a back green), these toughs often had sidelines in crime and frequently had goods which had 'fallen off a lorry'. Again many people, including respectable money conscious mothers, saw nothing wrong in paying cheaper rates for stolen property which they could not afford on the open market. They asked no questions and answered none. Even Boyle's mother (although 'straight' she had a weak, susceptible character) indulged in this practice and thought nothing of it. So for the youngster the twin threads of violence and crime took on a veneer of glamour and even necessity and certainly he saw nothing intrinsically wrong in taking the low road.

Street gangs were part of slumland sub-culture and it was inevitable that

Boyle would drift into one, in his case the 'Wild Young Cumbie' from Cumberland Street of which he became natural leader, and he excelled in pitched battles, at this stage mostly with fists, with neighbouring gangs. The admiration more timid urchins had for him increased with this and he had not even reached puberty.

His first defiant criminal acts were nothing more than surreptitiously stealing sweets and cakes from shop counters but from there he graduated to breaking into empty shops at night. Again his schoolmates thought these were great acts of derring-do.

When he was 13 he had his first confrontation with the law. He had gone on a spree of breaking into chewing gum machines with three of his mates but one of them was caught, broke down and told all. To Boyle's mother's naive amazement the family received a midnight visit from the constabulary and he was taken off, bubbling vociferously, to spend the night in a Young Offenders Institution. Here for the first time he was made to strip and put on uniform garb, had his fingerprints and photograph taken and his name was entered on police files, a document which was to grow to the size of a book over the years.

At the Central Police Court he appeared in the dock for the first time and was given two years probation after he swore that there would be no more trouble, sir.

Shortly after this he made a half hearted attempt to escape the Gorbals but only got as far as Edinburgh where he was found by a night security guard sleeping in a goods wagon. He then concentrated on shoplifting and stealing crates from brewers' lorries and he found no difficulty in getting rid of the goods. Quite the opposite. The demand was greater than the supply. But the police met up with him again when he was caught breaking into a hut to steal show pigeons and he was given two weeks detention.

On his release the routine began again: gang fights, breaking into shops and warehouses, caught, twenty eight days.

The violence always inherent in Boyle's nature now took a more serious turn and for the first time he started carrying a bayonet. In numerous gang fights on waste ground in the area he wielded this weapon indiscriminately, inflicting horrific injuries on his opponents while being spry enough to avoid serious injury himself. Most of his pals, and enemies, were likewise violent but even then he stood out for his reckless abandon in battle, what a Lord Advocate would later describe as "almost unimaginable ferocity", which was to mark him out as the most vicious of his violent fellows. The fact that his reputation among older criminals grew with every victory increased his bravado. In his own terms he was fast becoming the Young Pretender to the underworld's throne.

His thieving continued apace and it was while fleeing from the Kelvin Hall Carnival with a cash box that he was once more arrested. After serving a few months in an approved school he was allowed home. These periods of incarceration, after the initial shock had receded, did nothing to cure his criminality. Again the opposite happened: in these closed societies with the common enemy he was looked up to as a bit of a kingpin by those who felt rejected, downtrodden and forgotten. With his jaunty air it was easy for him to be superior even in these nether depths.

Once more he ran off, this time to the beckoning glories of London, was caught in a smash and grab raid and returned to approved school. After being released on probation he returned south once more and ran around with a mob of exiled Scottish hoodlums in the Kings Cross area, excelling himself to impress them in daring acts of robbery. He took to drinking heavily to emphasise his manhood, indulged in lengthy bouts of sex with prostitutes and dabbled in drugs. The streak of nihilism which scarred his life came to the fore at this time. His days were aimless, tomorrow held no meaning, relationships were empty unless based on bloody boasts and he did not give a damn about anything, especially life.

On his returns to the Gorbals he would bask in the reflected glories of his caperings in the Smoke and it was during one of these visits home that he was arrested for shopbreaking. This time it was Borstal for fourteen months. He was coming up in the world.

He found himself quite at home in this spartan world with its atmosphere of repressed violence - for many of his old chums were there. His sojourn did nothing to change his outlook on life except make him more depressive. It did help his criminal career, however, because on his and others' release he used the network of contacts he had built up to set himself up as a reseller of stolen goods. He also started a modest protection racket among pubs on the south side and took to carrying a Walther pistol in his waistband as well as his favourite bayonet rolled up in a copy of the *Glasgow Herald*. Borstal had taught him quite a lot.

However, his was not the only racket on the go and one night in Crown Street there was a full scale pitched battle with a rival gang in which he took his customary, expected leading part and the Royal Infirmary was kept busy treating the wounded casualties.

The Glasgow scene was now getting a bit too hot for Boyle so he retreated once more to London where he soon ended up in Wormwood Scrubs serving a six week sentence for police assault. Detectives met him at the gates on his release and he was taken to Glasgow High Court and found guilty of two charges of serious assault. This time it was Barlinnie Prison for two years. Even if he was only eighteen, he had come of age.

While inside he punched a prison officer who had insulted him and was put in solitary confinement for a fortnight which raised him in the esteem of many of the older lags. Barlinnie being the clearing ground for Glasgow's toughest criminals, whether they be en route to or from Peterhead or down for family visits, Boyle loved mixing and talking with these hard men and hearing tales of their prowess and vowed that when he got out he would make it big in crime. Reform never entered his head and as for the 'screws' they were merely objects of his hatred. He was one of the 94% of inmates who would never make it in the 'straight' world.

Physically at this time, Boyle was a stocky, well-built, cocky young man. He was good-looking with thick, black curly hair, a strong nose and jaw and features which could change instantly from jaunty, charming friendliness to cold ferocity.

He still had a reputation to live up to, so when the time came to step outside the prison gates some of his criminal cronies were there to greet him and let him know what was going on. Boyle was a willing listener and only too eager to join the newest criminal outfit - the Tallymen, whose leader was a Gorbals villain named Frank 'Tarzan' Wilson - as their chief heavy.

Their racket was simple. They loaned money, no questions asked or collateral needed, to whoever wanted it, repayable within an agreed time - at twenty five per cent interest. If the repayment was not forthcoming in time the interest went up ten per cent. If the borrower did not respond, Boyle was sent in and made sure, if the money could not be paid, that others were shown an example of what would happen if they did not play the game. Sometimes it was alcohol that customers needed, especially on Sundays when the pubs were shut, and the Tallymen kept their own stock. They were given their nickname because they went about with books in which the name and customer's tally was kept. Their favourite hunting grounds were the pubs and the thickset, smiling moneylenders with their wads of notes found the impoverished inebriated easy meat.

Boyle was the perfect strongarm man for the gang, even if he went about his task too enthusiastically at times. Only he knows how many customers he beat up, brutalised and terrorised at this time and, naturally enough, he is not saying. The majority of his victims were too scared to implicate him and many never even went to a doctor for fear of getting further involved. It has been estimated that Boyle's own league table of assaults was between eighty and a hundred, which gives an idea of the scale of the enterprise, and there was a rumour at one time, never properly substantiated, that he had crucified a customer to the floor of his home. Be that as it may, for every victim there were a dozen more ready to repay their debts even if it took months of handing over money to achieve this. Although the police knew what was going on they were frustrated at the impossibility of mustering enough jittery witnesses to make a case stand up in court.

In his spare time Boyle was also involved as a bouncer at shebeens and brothels throughout the south side where he freely partook of the available products. He was now approaching that peak of popularity he had always dreamt of in his murky imagination.

In December 1964 all that was threatened when he was arrested for the murder of a man named Lynch who had been a customer of the Tallymen. He was also charged with robbing Lynch and slashing a second man. But the usual frustrating problems of finding witnesses and corroborative evidence faced the police and at the High Court trial in March 1965 the charges were withdrawn and Boyle, beaming all over, marched down the court steps where he was mobbed by his cronies and the Press. He accepted an invitation into the *Daily Express* car but when the photographer later went into a phone box to phone his office Boyle followed him and presented a knife, slipped to him by a crony, at the photographer's throat threatening that if he was not promised "a lot of dough" for his story the photographer would be cut there and then. When told nothing would be forthcoming Boyle grudgingly let him go.

His reputation as the man who could freely commit murder, his place of honour in the underworld, had now been achieved. He was feted in Gorbals pubs by all the villains of the day, held in awe by the weak, spoken respectfully to by the cautious, the darling of the girls, the king of the hoodlums. For a while life was one big party, it was drinks on the house all the time and the police were furious at his effrontery.

But he still could not keep out of trouble and only ten days after his release he was involved in a fight with two other hoodlums who had mistakenly decided to take this big-head on and at the same time make a name for themselves. Defending himself with a broken bottle, Boyle gouged one of their eyes out and almost severed the hand of the other.

While on the run from this he attended a party in a city centre tenement which ended in a free-for-all with knives, bottles and glasses being used as weapons, the end result being two brothers stabbed, one fatally, and a series of multiple injuries. Boyle was arrested when he carelessly and drunkenly returned to his mother's house and he was charged with murder and three serious assaults.

But again witnesses were not forthcoming. The lights had gone out. Everyone was fighting each other. No-one could be certain about anything. The Procurator Fiscal announced that the murder charge against Boyle would be held "in abeyance" for the moment, the first time this had ever happened in a murder trial.

Just in case any of the witnesses had ideas about getting their memories back, one of their houses was blown up by a gelignite bomb while she was out shopping.

At the trial in October 1965 the murder charge was withdrawn but Boyle pled guilty to a reduced charge of pushing and jostling and was given a mere three months. This was tantamount to a second escape from life imprisonment and the villains talked admiringly about the lad's lucky star even more.

On his release he returned to the Tallymen and found business was booming as ever. Not all the profits were squandered, much of it being used to subsidise ancillary crime projects. The gang were now so confident of immunity that they took to carrying around guns and there were several shooting incidents with rivals who wanted to chisel in on the bonanza.

The Kray twins were busy building up their crime empire in Soho and Ronnie, through a contact named Big Pat Connolly, made several visits to Glasgow to hire hit men to do flying jobs for them. His favourite was Boyle although sometimes even Ronnie, always wanting a front of respectability and sophistication, became a trifle alarmed at some of the wild Scotsman's methods.

When the Kray's rival gang leaders in Soho, the Richardson brothers, were shot in the kneecaps, Scotland Yard were tipped off that it was two top Scots boys who had flown down on contract to do the job, returning home the same day. But no names were forthcoming. The 'Scots boys' also developed a penchant for crossbows which they would use on whoever opened the door of the intended victim, whether it was the right man or not. And they were linked with the disappearance of Mad Axeman Frank Mitchell whom the Krays 'sprung' from Dartmoor as a vainglorious prank before getting rid of him when he became an embarrassment.

Boyle did not just visit the Krays on business. He often went south on holiday or when he felt the Glasgow C.I.D. were annoying him too much and getting on his nerves.

He was now confident of his abilities, sure that he had the scene under control by use of his bayonet, with the top mob in command and the customers keeping the cash flowing. But his life was one of danger and mayhem and although he was riding high he must have known deep in his pessimistic soul that it could not last. Nothing ever had lasted.

His downfall came in the spring of 1967. He and another villain called William Wilson, 'Tarzan's' brother, on a wet, blustery night visited the Kinning Park flat of a pimp known as 'Babs' Rooney who owed the Tallymen the money. A drunken argument arose over non-payment and Rooney was fatally stabbed in the chest. The pair ran off but when word spread that the police had found his fingerprints on a beer can in the kitchen of Rooney's house Boyle fled south to the Smoke where his old pals the Krays hid him in a 'safe' house. But after a couple of months he made the arrogant mistake of summoning three of his Gorbals henchmen for a conference in a London pub. They were followed by C.I.D. men determined he would not get away this time. A large furniture van drew up outside the pub and suddenly the place was swarming with armed police and, manacled and furious, Boyle was escorted back to Glasgow.

However, he was not too despondent, confident that his pals on the outside would help rig the evidence, get at witnesses and get him off the hook as they had in the past. He was further heartened when he was told, as had happened before, that a gelignite bomb had exploded outside the house of a witness who had seen him in the vicinity of 'Babs' Rooney's flat at the time of the murder.

He went for trial at Glasgow High Court before Lord Cameron and security was strict with armed police in the building and others with walkie-talkie sets on surrounding rooftops.

Gradually, the evidence mounted - the bloodstained murder weapon found under the linoleum of his house, brave witnesses who testified that they had seen him flee the scene. But key witness Mrs. Sadie Cairney, who was 'Babs' Rooney's blonde girlfriend, and had been in his house at the time of his murder, swore on oath that it had been a stranger and not the accused who had killed her lover. Boyle smiled but at this crucial stage there was an adjournment during which, under police pressure, Sadie broke down in the cells under the court and admitted she had been intimidated and had lied.

After the recess, the Crown Prosecutor asked for Sadie, who had technically finished her evidence, to be allowed to go back into the box: but Lord Cameron turned this down. However, the jury could see Sadie sitting crying between two policewomen in the public benches and it was obvious to all and sundry what was afoot.

The Prosecutor made an eloquent speech and the jury retired for two hours. Boyle was finally doomed – guilty, unanimously. Lord Cameron then described him as a menace to society and sentenced him to life imprisonment with a recommendation that he serve not less than fifteen years. All the top brass of Glasgow police were there in the public benches and shook hands with each other.

The intimidation machine which Boyle's gang had successfully used for years had finally failed. At its most sophisticated it had worked through the gang's own crooked lawyer, James Maxwell Latta, a respectable but ambitious middle-aged father of three whose twin hobbies were collecting antique pistols and mixing with unsavoury underworld types. It was this slumming which was his undoing because he found it easier to bribe and threaten witnesses than live up to his professional code of conduct and he loved the kudos attached to getting guilty men off, being prepared to stake his livelihood and freedom for the glories of appearing to be

Glasgow's Clarence Darrow. His 'interview room' was often a bar in the Gorbals, the 'Hi-Hi', where, along with sundry colourful characters like Boyle, 'Tarzan' Wilson and 'Bandit' Rooney, evidence was concocted and he was also handed *ex gratia* payments to be the crooks' lawyer in court.

Following Boyle's murder of 'Babs' Rooney and subsequent conviction, Latta was jailed for eight years for trying to induce Sadie to say it had been one of two unknown men in light raincoats who had come to her home in Kinning Park and killed Rooney and not Boyle.

Lord Grant, passing sentence, told Latta, "There is no doubt that the administration of justice in Glasgow has been suffering over recent years because witnesses - whether persuaded or intimidated - have failed to give truthful evidence. It has been a crying scandal.

"Furthermore, the tracking down and conviction of the perpetrators, the instigators, is a difficult and, in many cases, impossible task."

Lord Grant then told the city's senior magistrate who was in court to hear sentence being passed, "I believe we have been bedevilled in Glasgow in past years, time and again, by acquittals which have resulted in guilty men going free because witnesses have been tampered with, intimidated, and false evidence given.

"That, I believe, is the experience of every judge who has sat here in recent years and, probably, though I cannot speak with first hand knowledge, of most counsel."

It was a frank admission of the power of the Tallymen but now their reign of terror was over. With the threat of Boyle lifted, other ringleaders and their cohorts were rounded up and jailed on various charges ranging from intimidation and extortion to serious assault and attempting to pervert the course of justice. 'Tarzan', the brain behind the whole operation, was given twelve years.

Although now inside for life, Boyle's hatred had by no means run its course. He gave the Governor in Barlinnie an uppercut which sent him flying off his seat and broke his cheekbone, an offence for which he was given a severe beating and a further eighteen months. His preliminary hearing in front of a Sheriff on this charge was unique in that it took place in cells under the court and he was surrounded by armed police. (It was also like a military operation when he was allowed to attend his mother's funeral in the Gorbals several months later with van loads of armed police surrounding the cemetery.)

On arriving at Peterhead Prison he assaulted two prison officers, biting one of them and punching the other, for which he received four years. At Porterfield Prison in Inverness (nicknamed Siberia among prisoners) he and others were involved in a scrap with prison officers during which there was much punching and kicking for which he received a month in solitary confinement.

This violent catalogue of numerous assaults on prison officers, and occasionally prisoners, continued for five bloodstained years and for most of that time Boyle was confined to solitary and received a dozen hammerings from the 'batter squads' in Peterhead, Barlinnie and Porterfield. None of them wanted him, none of them could contain or repress him, he was labelled as uncontrollable and the lengthier his barbaric record became the less he seemed to care. He only wanted to inflict pain and suffering, to hit back, to take as many 'screws' with him as possible.

The first solution the prison authorities came up with only made the situation worse and led to tragedy. They reasoned, in a narrow, blinkered way, that if Boyle insisted on acting like an animal then they would treat him like one. They penned him in a specially constructed block at Porterfield Prison which became notorious as 'The Cages'. These were six cells and within each was a small cage.

Boyle, stark naked, was kept in one of these cages which was hardly big enough for a large dog to turn around in. There was a two inch gap which opened at feeding time and food was shoved through as if to a creature in a zoo. There were no toilet facilities whatsoever, no furniture, nothing. Opaque glass and heavy wire mesh deliberately made it impossible to tell if it was day or night. A dim light burned all the time. 'The Cages' were designed to degrade and dehumanise and they succeeded.

For two hours a week the prisoners were allowed into a small recreation room. The place was a time bomb and for someone like Boyle a spark was all that was needed.

There are two versions of the riot which took place on the evening of December 28th 1972 in the recreation room. The prison officers' official version claimed that it was a pure and simple attempt to escape and that they were attacked by the prisoners without warning and had to fight for their lives.

The prisoners version is that they had sat down and linked arms in a peaceful protest against 'The Cages' when they were suddenly set upon by the prison officers and had to defend themselves.

Either way the room erupted into a mini battlefield with batons splintering, knives flashing and blood gushing as four prisoners and six prison officers desperately fought each other. It was claimed the prisoners had in their possession a rope of sheets, three knives, a weighted sock and a radio which it was presumed would be used to monitor news of their escape once they got over the wall. How they were supposed to have acquired these implements was a mystery which neither side could or would clear up.

Boyle, of course, was named as the self-appointed ringleader and the others were Howard Wilson, serving life (see chapter 7), Larry Winters, serving life, and William McPherson, serving 25 years. Boyle, according to the staff, kept screaming, "Kill, kill, kill!" and stabbed one prison officer, who was a former professional boxer, fifteen times before he was overpowered and beaten unconscious. Another prison officer lost an eye in the melee and another one, who was stabbed three times, had to struggle through a rain of blows before he could press the alarm bell. He said later that he had been flattened by a chair then saw Winters advancing towards him "in slow motion with a smile on his face", before the door burst open and help arrived.

Boyle almost lost his life over this riot following the sustained and systematic beating he received once he had been hauled back to his cage. A doctor who later examined him said he was surprised he had lasted the night. He was like a carcass of raw meat.

At the trial held at Inverness High Court, again with massive security precautions, the four prisoners were found not guilty of attempting to murder the six prison officers but all were found guilty of assaulting five officers and attempting to escape. They were all sentenced to an additional six years.

Before the sentence was passed Boyle asked if he could address the judge, Lord Wheatley, on his own behalf. This was refused but through his counsel he was allowed to say that he considered he had been brutally treated and severely injured but that he felt it had all been worthwhile as it had brought their grievances to light.

Twelve of the 55 prison officers at Porterfield resigned after the riot, including some of those involved.

The prison authorities now decided to try a new tack with Boyle. Word filtered through that he was to be transferred to a new Special Unit that was to be opened up at Barlinnie. At this stage only the Home and Health Department knew what this Unit was to do and Boyle was very alarmed since there were rumours that it was to be a cross between a prison and a psychiatric ward and he feared he was going to be drugged or lobotomised into subjection. It had been nicknamed the 'Nutcracker Suite'.

But after he had got over the first shock of not being assaulted, of being able to walk around and do the toilet without being supervised, of being able to wear his own clothes, of being addressed as 'Jimmy' by the friendly prison officers, he became the Unit's star inmate. He was now being treated as a human being and from being a cornered animal he was transformed into a creative personality.

The Unit, which operated until 1994, was based on the principle of self reliance, of giving the prisoners what Boyle describes as "a sense of freedom" within the confines of four walls. Weekly meetings were held at which the inmates put forward suggestions to improve conditions. They could criticise the staff and if any of the inmates stepped out of line he was put in the 'hot seat' and asked to justify his actions or apologise. The inmates did their own cooking and ate round a communal table. They were allowed to study educational courses, had a television and radios and were granted regular visits from friends and relatives. Books and writing materials were freely available.

Prison officers throughout Scotland heaved a sigh of relief that at long last Boyle was out of the system and, after his move to the Unit, the serious trouble in Scottish prisons considerably calmed down.

Thanks to the visit of an art teacher Boyle, who had also been taking a correspondence course in psychology, found he had a talent for sculpting clay and some of his work, with clenched fists and chains a recurrent theme, went on display in an Edinburgh gallery. Boyle was allowed out for the day under supervision to attend this exhibition, an occasion which almost reduced him to tears.

In addition, he collaborated with playwright Tom McGrath in writing a drama about his experiences in prison, particularly in 'The Cages', which was titled *The Hard Man* and which was performed throughout Britain.

Boyle also wrote his memoirs, aptly titled *A Sense of Freedom*, which deal at great detailed length with prison brutality while being an apologia for his own atrocious crimes. So much of his long criminal career is glossed over or whitewashed that this part of the book is worse than worthless: it is downright misleading. Nevertheless, considering the nature of the author it is a remarkable achievement.

In September 1977 the future of the Unit was threatened with the death of inmate Larry Winters. He was found dead in his cell, his naked corpse sitting on a chamber pot, and a post mortem revealed he had died of an overdose of tranquillis-ers. His relatives later claimed it was easy to get drugs, drink and sex in the Unit and said women were free to visit the prisoners in their cells. No solid evidence was found to support these allegations but, nevertheless, as a result of Winters' death security was severely tightened and there were changes in staff.

Amidst the hysteria it was forgotten that Winters' death was particularly poignant because he had shown the makings of being a writer and poet as well as being expert on the guitar. He died at the age of 34, having been in prison for 13 years, two of them in solitary confinement. A toughened character in the Boyle mould, he had been one of the first 'lifers' after the abolition of capital punishment. Since he had held up and shot a barman he would almost certainly have been 'topped' in the old days. After his death, scraps of manuscripts were collected from the Special Unit and published under the title *The Silent Scream*. One example will give a taste of his bitter, garish style.

ELECTRIC DREAMS
the dream goes on
       through winding sandstone streets
where bewildered ancient gas-lamps & cracked paves
look on as the electric drunk & his favourite sword
baffle the Bluesteel guards & the red-eyed Boar
the dream goes on
      in derelict tenements the Python coils
& wild wolves howl through the crystal film
& shadows mask the mouldering walls
    the dream goes on
& the dream goes on ...
    tiers
        of tears &
lobotomised heads
    empty smiles
& bluefaced guards with tranquil guns
ah the dream goes on
    with E.C.T &
brainbursting drugs &
faceless men in soothing suits
sit silent sit silent silent
& the dream goes on
    of plastic plates &
rubber knives & hollow heads hanging
ah weary the watchful walls
    weary and wistful the wings void
of woe the warder whistles
    & the dream goes on ...

Chapter six:
DANCING WITH DEATH

The most extensive and longest manhunt in Scottish criminal history took place in the late sixties and centred on a shadowy, elusive figure- who haunted a brassy Glasgow ballroom. He was an immaculate, well groomed gent who was well spoken, polite and, possibly, even religious. He was light on his feet, a good dancer and his charm was literally fatal. It was a case in which the police received massive nationwide help, had all the advantages of modern forensic science at their fingertips, as much evidence as any detective could pray for and a murderer who picked the most public of places, a dance hall, where people went deliberately to eye up others - and yet that final clue proved as difficult to pinpoint as the man who terrorised the city.

At that time the Barrowland Ballroom just east of the city's High Street was a popular night spot where the dance floor was nightly packed, the music loud and lively, the atmosphere raucous and abandoned and, in the shadows round the walls, jabbed occasionally by neon lights, the eyes of the boys on the town hungrily eyed up the 'talent'. On Thursday, Friday and Saturday nights of the week it was well known that bored married women took off their rings, popped them in their handbags and loosened up for a spree and a bit of fun. On these occasions it was easy pickings for any presentable young man out for a night's sex.

It was on the night of Friday February 23rd 1968 that a vivacious 25-year-old brunette called Pat Docker was gyrating to the music in a sexy black dress and letting herself go after a busy week at the Victoria Infirmary where she worked as a nurse. She danced with several young men in the semi-darkness that night but no-one could later recall in whose arms she enjoyed the last waltz.

The following morning, a Saturday, some boys were playing in a lane beside Pat's home in Carmichael Place, Langside, when they saw what at first glance appeared to be a broken tailor's dummy lying on the ground. On investigation the grim truth was obvious. It was the stark naked, strangled body of a girl.

It did not take the police long to establish that the dead girl, who had been throttled with her own tights and raped, was Pat Docker. Her distraught father identified her.

Nor did it take them long to discover that a press photographer had been holding a large, noisy party, attended by nurses, in his nearby flat. Detectives took over editors' offices in newspapers throughout the city and interviewed everyone who had been at the party, much to the embarrassment of some of the reporters who were supposed to have been touring the police stations in radio cars on calls duty that night.

But no clues were forthcoming, no-one had seen or heard anything suspicious and, anyway, Pat almost certainly was not at the party but was down in the lane with someone. Her clothes and handbag were never found and, despite intensive investigations lasting months, neither was her murderer.

Business at the Barrowland continued as usual until the night of Saturday

August 16th of the following year when slim, dark haired 32-year-old Jemima McDonald, an unmarried mother of three, decided to let herself loose at one of the dance hall's notorious swinging singles nights. She too wore a black dress and enjoyed herself, laughing and drinking and getting up with whoever asked.

She left the dance hall with a man and walked in the direction of her older sister's house in Mackeith Street, Bridgeton, where she had arranged to spend the night. But when she failed to arrive back the sister became alarmed in the early hours and decided to go out looking for her. It did not take her long to find Jemima's body which lay sprawled on derelict property a few yards away.

Death was due to strangulation by her own tights and she had also been raped. Her handbag was missing. Apart from the other coincidences with the Docker murder - the dance hall, each having dark hair and dresses, each young, attractive and available, each meeting their deaths in the same way and having their bags stolen - both women had been having their periods.

But this time the police seemed to be on better ground. They had a description. Several people had seen Jemima leave with her last partner and they had both been seen strolling through the midnight streets.

The police assembled an Identikit picture and issued it to the press, the first time this had been done in Scotland. It showed the pleasant, well balanced face of a clean shaven, fresh faced man in his late twenties with dark eyes and short, brushed back reddish fair hair. In addition, he was described as being six feet tall of slim build and immaculately dressed in a blue suit of good quality with hand stitched lapels and a white shirt. If this was indeed the man then one could well imagine women finding him attractive and allowing themselves to be escorted away by him.

As in the Docker case the police appealed to patrons of the dance hall to come forward but they had to deal with the frustrating problem that many of the dancers were wives who should not have been there in the first place and who had no intention of getting involved. Only a smattering of staff and dancers who had nothing to hide volunteered statements and they could add nothing to the description. Not quite certain yet if there was any connection with the Docker case the police nevertheless went over every possible angle - relatives, friends, possible motives of any boyfriends - with their usual painstaking thoroughness and the investigation was still continuing when the thunderbolt really struck.

Mother of two Mrs. Helen Puttock, a chubbily attractive 29-year-old brunette whose husband was serving in the Army, was not bothered by press theories that there might be a strangler on the loose at the Barrowland Ballroom, knowing as she did that it could never happen to her and, anyway, she was a good judge of character. Ten weeks after the McDonald murder, on Thursday 30th October, she too decided to go out for a night on the tiles and she too, apparently, could have danced all night in her sexy black dress at the ballroom.

She went with her sister, Mrs. Jean Langford, and in the dimness of the hall she tried to get some cigarettes from a machine which jammed. A well dressed young man stepped forward and offered to help get her money back and the two got into conversation. They then had a drink and a dance, he said he would see her home (you couldn't be too careful these days) and towards midnight they met Mrs.

Langford, who was leaving. The three got into a taxi to Scotstoun where the sisters lived and Mrs. Langford was dropped off at her home before the taxi went on to near Helen's house in Earl Street where she and her well-spoken, new found friend, who was called John, alighted. It was the last time anyone, except John, was to see her alive.

The next morning a woman emptying out rubbish found Helen's corpse in a back court a few closes from the dead woman's home. She had been strangled with her tights and raped, her bag was missing and she, too, had been having her periods. The hue and cry now really began in earnest.

Thanks to Mrs. Langford and the taxi driver the police now not only had a minutely detailed description of the murder suspect but also facts about John's background which he had revealed in the taxi.

First the physical description, which was possibly the most accurate in Scottish criminal history. It was issued by Detective-Chief Superintendent Elphinstone Dalglish, then head of Glasgow C.I.D.

John was clean shaven, in his late twenties, six feet tall of slim to medium build with light auburn reddish hair styled short and brushed to the right, all of which fitted with the last man seen with Jemima McDonald. In addition, he had blue grey eyes, nice straight teeth with one tooth on the right upper jaw overlapping the next tooth, fine features and was of smart appearance. On the night he met Helen he was dressed in a brownish, flecked, single breasted suit, the jacket of which had three buttons and high lapels. There were no turn-ups on the trousers and the suit generally was in modern style. He also wore a knee length brown coat of tweed or gaberdine, a light blue shirt and a dark tie with red diagonal stripes. He had a wrist watch with a broad leather strap of military style and smoked Embassy tipped cigarettes. He frequented the Barrowland Ballroom on his own. He could have had scratch marks on his face and hands as a result of his attack on Helen.

As to his background, he had a sister and had been brought up strictly by his puritanical parents who were very religious and teetotal and who had vainly tried to instill in him a dislike for alcohol. He could quote extracts from the Bible. He was well spoken despite a Glasgow accent and did not appear to be engaged in heavy manual work. He could play golf but was not very good at it although a cousin had recently scored a hole-in-one. He was, a bachelor who lived with a relative, probably in the Castlemilk area of Glasgow. He was personable, handsome and probably occupied some place in society where he had some authority. It was this respectable, clean-cut image which helped protect him.

An evening newspaper news editor now dubbed the murderer 'Bible John' and the name caught the public imagination and stuck. The heat was now on the police to come up with results.

There had only been two recent manhunts in the city comparable to it. One was for the Box Man, a pederast who preyed on young boys in the Partick district by saying he had a present for them in a box thus enticing them into a backcourt where he would bugger them. And the other for a labourer in the St. George's Cross area who would take little girls into back closes and sexually assault them with a chisel. Both were pathological sexual perverts who otherwise led normal lives and despite large-scale police investigations and 'sex patrols' both had only been caught by luck, one running away from an assault and the other through a suspicious workmate. But both were dwarfed by the massive Bible John hunt.

The police now had a second picture of Bible John following Helen's murder but this time, instead of using the Identikit method, they took the unusual step of hiring an artist to paint a portrait of the wanted man. It was broadly similar to the Jemima McDonald murder picture and showed a very presentable young man who looked as though he could be trusted. Tens of thousands of these posters were distributed in public places throughout Scotland and to police forces throughout Britain as well as to military units abroad.

Detectives now definitely and openly linked all three murders and a Bible John H.Q., was set up in the Marine Police Station, Helen's murder having taken place in its area. More than a hundred detectives were assigned to the case and forces throughout the country were asked to co-operate. More than fifty thousand statements were taken in door-to-door inquiries or volunteered from members of the public, from taxi drivers, bus drivers, dancers and dance hall managers and staff, publicans, hoteliers, anyone involved with religious groups like the Mormons, ministers and priests, religious seminaries and colleges, nurses, newspapermen and much of the huge sprawling estate of Castlemilk was 'checked out'. Records were methodically examined, lunatic asylums visited, prisons and borstals visited, state hospitals visited. Barber shops were visited and asked about John's hairstyle and golf clubs held special meetings attended and addressed by senior detectives in an attempt to place John and his elusive cousin's hole-in-one. Dentists were asked to check their chart records and Helen's distraught husband, discharged from the Army to look after his two little sons, offered a personal reward of £200 for information at a specially organised police press conference. The Armed Forces were thoroughly checked and detectives travelled to NATO countries to see if suitable leave passes coincided with the murders. The Special Investigation Branches of the Army, Navy and Air Force travelled throughout the world, even as far as Hong Kong, during the investigation and gradually, with masses of statements, documents and photographs piling up, the murder H.Q., where a special 24 hour switchboard was installed, began to take on the appearance of a mini British Museum.

The media were constantly badgered to appeal for information and there was a unique BBC documentary compiled, with the Lord Advocate's blessing, which graphically reconstructed the night of Helen's murder. The part of John was portrayed by an upholsterer who had been interviewed but cleared by the police and the roles of the dead woman and her sister were taken by policewomen who looked similar. There was even a dramatic appeal over the air by commentator Hugh Cochrane which was couched in Biblical terms and asked John for his sins to give himself up. This programme alone brought a flood of a thousand calls to the murder H.Q.

Even the underworld offered its services. The stepping up of police checks, raids, patrols and general intensification of investigations into the criminal element was making life distinctly uncomfortable for several dubious characters and, anyway, villains generally have a deep-rooted antipathy for the lone wolf slayers of women or sexual perverts - not just because the underworld has its human side too but also because they give crime a bad name and can make routine 'jobs' more difficult (as was the case with the Manuel murders). But here the underworld came up against the same problem as the police - the killer apparently had no record and was not one of their number so how could they track him down? Solemn conversations in the back rooms of pubs, mini summit conferences in certain slumland houses and various messages tapped out on the underworld grapevine brought no results and villains had to stoically suffer the police harassment and sit out the manhunt in the hope that the killer could be caught by more conventional and official detection methods.

But the hunt had its humorous side too. One gentleman, a printer, was one of several young men who had the misfortune to be the double of one of the posters. He became sick fed up with conscientious passers-by making citizen's arrests and dragging him off to the nearest police station as he protested his innocence. On one occasion he was calmly walking along a city street when he suddenly found himself face down on the pavement with his legs trapped. A husky citizen had him pinned in a rugby tackle. This was the last straw and, knowing that the police had cleared him at the outset, he insisted that the Chief Constable give him a signed certificate saying he was not, definitely not, Bible John.

Many innocent men had the embarrassment and misfortune to be interviewed by the police and be told people had always had their suspicions about them and many a one became distinctly uneasy when being stared at while sitting in buses or trains and later being followed by alert citizens, not to mention downright cranks.

And a night out at the Barrowland Ballroom could be an amusing activity at this time. The murders had meant a decline in business but the floor was still packed, except many of the dancers were exceptionally well groomed and behaved. They were all P.C.s and W.P.C.s in plain if fashionable clothes and anyone who was not had the uncomfortable feeling of dozens of pairs of eyes sizing them up. The murder squad was christened the Marine Police Formation Team and one detective said on the TV documentary, "We must be the best dancers in the country by now. We are there at least twice a week and this has been going on for months. But people must think we are strange. We don't look at the women but the men."

And as the months went by without success at least one senior detective had to be given sick leave because he would leap from his car in the middle of traffic to grab and interview neat young men on the spot before summarily clearing them after a few minutes of questioning. And when asked what he wanted for Christmas he growled at his wife, "Bible John - in wrapping paper!"

The end result of all this frenetic activity, with all the modern aids to detection in full use, was - nothing. The file is still open. Every time a sexual murder is committed the ghost rears up once more but so far as is known there were only three Bible John murders.

Or were there only two? One theory was that the first, the Pat Docker murder, was separate because she was naked and her clothes were never found, suggesting she had been murdered in a house and dumped in the lane. The murderer would hardly have taken the time and trouble and risk of discovery involved in stripping her in the lane and she would not have voluntarily been naked in the open air in mid-February. Yet all the other coincidences would suggest it was the same man, even if the murder did not actually take place in the lane.

Of course, there were plenty of theories. One was that he died after the last murder - but a healthy young man does not simply die because he has committed murder. Another solution put forward was suicide but no reports of this fitted. He emigrated, he was shut up in an asylum, he was imprisoned - take your pick.

The police were probably thrown off the scent by the two identity pictures. The only people who saw him for any length of time did so in places of semi-darkness, a dance hall, a street, a taxi - and, as was proved, the main features could fit an awful lot of men. And it is well known that witnesses under pressure from the police will agree that his eyes were like this or his nose was like that, just to get some peace.

As regards the statements he made about himself, if he was astute enough and deliberately planning a murder, he could invent a false background for himself to throw witnesses and the police completely off the scent. But it still seems more likely that the statements were true and that he had no preconceived aim of killing but did so in the frenzy of the moment.

Sexual murderers with no records are the most difficult to catch and luck is needed by the police. On this occasion the dice rolled for Bible John.

Over the years there have been numerous false alarms about the case being solved, most notably when a soldier with a violent history who had committed suicide was exhumed from a Lanarkshire graveyard, using a mechanical digger in midwinter, so that his DNA could be compared with evidence still left in storage from the 1960s - but the results proved either negative or inconclusive and certainly did not offer an end to the mystery.

Instead there have been as many theories about Bible John as there were about Jack the Ripper, the most outlandish being that in fact ther were three separate killers who just happened to have the same modus operandi. Meanwhile, all those directly involved in the case have gradually passed on over the years, finally erasing their vital first hand testimony forever. Unless some extremely unlikely deathbed confession turns up, it looks as though John - or whatever his name was - got away with it.

Chapter seven:
ON THE MAKE

There is nothing more pathetic than the downfall of a bright and good young man whose ambition if properly tethered would have made him a success but who goes sadly awry and brings disaster - not only to himself but also to innocent people around him. This was the case with Howard Wilson, at one time a bright spark in the Glasgow Police whose desperate expectations ended in a bloodbath. Starting off as someone who always wanted to be different, above the rest, he ended up a total outcast, banished by his fellows on both sides of the law and left to revolve the rest of his days round the black void that used to be his life.

Impatience allied to ambition proved his fatal flaw. Many policemen become disillusioned with their job, the strict regimentation, the uniformity, the necessity of always having to obey, the long hours for indifferent pay, having to mingle with the garbage of society while having to suffer abuse and physical violence, while at home wives wait and worry. It is a vocation. It requires dedication. It needs restraint.

Of those who fall by the wayside some simply leave for employment elsewhere. But others become tainted with the corruption they daily deal with and the open sore of cynicism poisons their outlook on life. With Wilson, the bitterness was deeper than most and when he turned his back on the law he not only ended up hitting back at society which he thought had cornered him but he hit back with a vengeance at the symbols of that establishment which he felt had rejected him:

Wilson, the son of a newsagent, came of a respectable family with no criminal history. He was educated at Glasgow Academy and in December 1958 he joined Glasgow Police. He had always wanted to be in the force and nurtured dreams of being a top crimebuster like Sir Percy Sillitoe and with his keen intelligence, athletic body and driving enthusiasm, prospects seemed exceedingly good. But his was the sort of snap-to-attention, eager-to-please approach which can backfire if it comes up against a slow, orthodox method of career advancement. In other areas, kudos and promotion can be won quickly by spectacular successes but with the police, who naturally put great store by years of experience in their higher echelons, the process takes time and as Wilson saw some of his non-police chums driving about in sporty cars and natty suits he became gradually dissatisfied with the routine paperwork and petty offences that were his lot. It seemed that the day he would be cracking those big cases and getting in the headlines receded with every plodding step he took forward. He began to think his superiors were thick and narrow minded in not recognising his undoubted capabilities. Although only in his twenties, he became restless and realised that if he had to change course it would have to be soon or he would be stuck in the force, possibly doomed to be always in uniform for the rest of his working life. Gradually his talk in the locker room became more critical and he began to drift apart from his more patient colleagues.

Meanwhile during his fourth year in the force he married an attractive girl,

Julia, and the couple soon had two baby boys. This intensified the wish to improve his lot, now not only for himself but also for his family.

After several years on the beat - during which time he had to wait in ambush for killer James Boyle in the latter's house while he was on the run - Wilson thought things were at last looking up when he was given a job with promotion potential as a turnkey at the Central Police Office.

In his spare time he retained his school interest in rugby and played in the police team as prop forward. A team photograph of him at this time shows a grinning, broadfaced, seemingly happy man with a high intelligent forehead and receding thinning hair. There is nothing to suggest anything sinister. He looks just one of the boys.

He was also gregarious on social occasions and known as an ebullient cracker of jokes and a telling impersonator. He became a member of Bearsden Shooting Club and shared his interest in guns with fellow policeman John Sim (who also shared the same shifts at the Central) and prison officer Ian Donaldson. It was to prove a doomed friendship for the trio.

The Glasgow which Wilson patrolled in the sixties was a restless, changing environment which seemed full of new opportunities. The old tenements were being cleared away and new high-rise flats were taking their place. The city's population was declining. It had lost its right to be called the second city of the Empire, Birmingham's population of 1,112,000 beating it by 22,000. But where there used to be 500 people to the acre in Glasgow there was now new space in which to breathe and feel free. In addition, there was a fresh spirit about, there was new affluence, there was upward social mobility in careers, old taboos were being demolished along with decrepit buildings and it was said the bad days were gone forever. Heavy industry was declining but there was still plenty of work around in other areas and there were plenty of ambitious people 'swinging' with the times as in the rest of Britain.

But for Howard Wilson 1967 brought the sour taste of defeat. He was put back on the beat for no apparent reason. For a man who, throughout his nine years of service, had three times been commended by his Chief Constable for zeal and initiative it was the last straw. After a discussion with his wife, he resigned. It came as no surprise to his colleagues.

Fancying himself now as a small-time business entrepreneur who would build up a thriving chain of shops, he opened a greengrocers business near his home in Allison Street. Although now out of the force, Wilson frequently met his ex-colleagues because his ground floor flat in a gray tenement block was opposite Glasgow's Southern Police Station.

His former colleague John Sim had also become disillusioned with police work, for similar reasons to Wilson's, and had opened a garage service and Ian Donaldson, their friend in the shooting club, had left the prison service to become a motor mechanic.

But things began to go badly wrong for Wilson's presumed business acumen and he found trade was not as he had expected while his debts mounted rapidly. In conversation with Sim and Donaldson during their shooting practice he joked about the perfect crime, the one-off job, that could solve all his problems and after a while in the course of these gradually more serious talks he discovered the three of them had a factor in common - insurmountable debts and the prospect of ruin.

Each of them knew all about crime, how it was committed, how foolish mistakes led to capture, how with a bit of planning a job could be carried out with successful expertise. Wilson was now no longer the super detective; he was to be the arch criminal. Society had dealt him a lousy hand and he felt no regrets about hitting back to get himself out of the mess.

The robbery joke had now become a haunting reality and plans were laid for a big bank job. At his later trial Wilson's Q.C., Mr. Nicholas Fairbairn, eloquently stated that debt was a cruel and relentless master, creating in its victims the fantasy that one visit to Aladdin's cave would result in the terrible burden being gone forever "and so they took the fateful decision".

The target was the British Linen Bank in Eastwood - Mains Road, Giffnock, Renfrewshire. Wilson decided to bring in a fourth man on the job, his business partner in the greengrocer's shop, twenty-one-year-old Archibald McGeachie, who acted as driver in the raid, he being as desperate for money as Wilson. The raid took place on July 16th, 1969. Their faces covered by masks and wielding guns as well as bottles of ammonia they charged into the bank, threatened, tied up and blindfolded the staff before wrenching out phones, opening the safe and escaping clear in the revved up getaway car round the corner with £20,876 - all in a matter of minutes.

Cock-a-hoop with their perfect crime, the raiders calmly strode into Wilson's house opposite the police station and split up the loot.

But the euphoria did not last for long. True, Wilson and McGeachie paid off their debts on the grocery business and Sim and Donaldson settled their motoring commitments amicably: but after this had been done there was nothing left and the foursome's legitimate business expertise proved no more profitable than before and once again the spectre of mounting debts returned to haunt them.

Emboldened by the success of the bank raid, Wilson decided that just one more time would prove the clincher that would make them all a success and the dream of the good life - fat cigars, champagne, good food, a villa - kept him awake at night in his cramped flat. So he suggested to his accomplices another job but this time he came up against opposition from two of them.

Donaldson was not a man of violence and the prospect of another ordeal in a bank robbery frightened him: but, after persuasion and the promise that there would be no rough stuff, as well as the financial and emotional pressures imposed on him by his thalidomide daughter, he eventually nodded agreement.

The other dissenter was McGeachie and for Wilson he was a much harder obstacle to overcome. He was adamant that he wanted no part of any further job or indeed of Wilson. In addition McGeachie had not got rid of his spoils to the same extent as Wilson but yet at the same time he refused to help bail out his floundering business partner. Relations between the two men deepened into distrust, enmity and bitterness.

All that can be said about the hapless McGeachie is that he was never seen alive again after December 23rd, 1969. But his disappearance took a bizarre turn three years later when his parents claimed he had been murdered. They applied to the Court of Session in Edinburgh and as a result he was officially pronounced dead and it was announced he had left £9,432 according to a confirmation of his estate lodged with the Sheriff Clerk. Mr. McGeachie senior said he believed his son's murdered body had been buried by a labourer paid to carry out the grisly task in the concrete foundations of the multi-million-pound Kingston Bridge which was completed seven months after his disappearance. It proved scientifically impossible to confirm this, short of knocking down the bridge, but by that time more drastic events had superseded the disappearance of the amateur bank robber.

It was two days before the New Year that the fateful second job which was to cure all the robber's ills took place, twelve days after the abolition of hanging had gone through the House of Lords and seven days after McGeachie, who had known so much, had vanished. It was December 30th, 1969 cold and bleak with a widow's wind blowing icily, when Scotland was looking forward to the Hogmanay festivities and a feeling of light-heartedness was traditionally in the air.

The three well dressed men who quietly entered the Clydesdale Bank at Bridge Street, Linwood, Renfrewshire in the afternoon looked like ordinary customers there to pick up some cash before the bank closed for the holidays. The fact that they were carrying suitcases only reinforced the impression that they were no doubt going away over the holiday period and would need some money. When one of them, Sim, politely asked if he could open an account for a plant hire business he was ushered into the office of the assistant manager. But no sooner had the door closed than the assistant was flung to the floor and Sim pressed a pistol against his temple and hissed, "Listen, you will hear me release the safety catch!" Wilson held a knife at his throat and muttered, "If we have full co-operation no member of your staff will come to any harm!"

A pillow case was taken from a suitcase, put over the assistant manager's head and his hands were tied behind his back. The keys to the front door were located and the three men came out of the office, rounded up the other clerks and a customer and placed them, bound and hooded, beside the assistant before locking the front door. But one woman customer with her two-year-old son came to the door knocking urgently to get in as it was not yet closing time. Realising she could attract attention, the raiders let her in then glared at the startled woman and said that she had better behave or her baby would be shot. They then manhandled the youngest clerk and made him show them were the money was kept. The raiders began to fill suitcases and a box with money from the safe and counter drawers. Their greed to take silver coins as well as notes later proved to be their undoing. Again all the phones were ripped out before the three locked the manager's office then calmly walked to their car outside. None of the shoppers round about noticed anything unusual.

They returned as before to Wilson's house to split up the proceeds. They took the notes into the tenement without any bother. There was a discussion as to whether they should just leave the loose change in the car and sort it out later or risk being seen bringing it in. But they decided that the chance of being thought suspicious was remote and, besides, nothing had happened before because they reasoned their open brazenness allayed suspicions which shiftiness would arouse, and what was more to the point - the more money the better. However, they, with their thieves' instinct, did not trust just one to go out and get the rest of the loot so all three strolled out to the car.

Inspector Andrew Hyslop was driving towards the Southern Police Station at this precise moment. His colleague, Constable John Sellars, was in the squad car with him and they were returning from a routine patrol. The two policemen noticed the three men carrying suitcases into the close. Inspector Hyslop, knowing of Wilson's flagging greengrocery business, suspected he could be resetting stolen whisky. The police in Allison Street involved in the events to follow did not know of any bank robbery.

Inspector Hyslop went to the police station for assistance while Constable Sellars stopped Wilson at the close mouth. The bank robber said he was merely going to a shop nearby and that he himself was a former policeman. Constable Sellars returned to the squad car and was joined by Inspector Hyslop who had brought along Detective Constable Angus McKenzie, aged 30, and Constable Edward Barnett, aged 24, and a Constable Campbell. When Wilson returned with a bottle of lemonade he was asked about what he had been unloading into his house. Wilson was polite and co-operative and they all entered his house where he offered them a drink which was turned down. Inspector Hyslop opened a case and found it contained bags of cash stamped 'Linwood'. The officers now dispersed throughout the kitchen, bedroom and bathroom to see what else they could find. At the first arrival of the police Donaldson had escaped through a window while Sim had dumped a pistol in Wilson's bedroom wardrobe.

While the police were searching the house, Wilson slipped into the bed-room and, having found out from a terrified Sim where the gun was, he grabbed it and reappeared in the hallway to come face to face with Inspector Hyslop who had just emerged from searching the bathroom.

Wilson raised his right extended arm and aimed at the frozen policeman's head. He was later to tell fellow prisoners that he would never forget those seconds and the astonished look in the eyes of Inspector Hyslop as he stared at death.

Wilson tried to fire but there was a click indicating that the pistol had jammed. He pulled back the sliding jacket to clear the obstruction and aimed again but by this time the Inspector had gained his senses and was rushing at him. But it was too late and a bullet struck him on the left side of the face, spinning him round. He fell to the floor, paralysed but still fully conscious.

It was later said in Wilson's defence that he had no sensible recollection of using the gun, that he was numb with fear, irrational, shouting and yelling without meaning, the whites of his eyes blazing and that he was in an uncontrollable state. That was not so. He had a clear idea of what he was going to do (he had probably formulated it while going for the lemonade). He was going to kill all the officers and dump their bodies and car in a loch or shoot himself in the process since life would hardly be worth living anyway.

While Inspector Hyslop lay helpless staring at the horror unfolding a few feet away from him, Detective Constable MacKenzie rushed into the hall from the living room and Constable Barnett appeared at the kitchen door. Wilson aimed with his marksman's precision and accurately shot MacKenzie in the head before swing-ing round on Barnett and shooting the startled constable again on target in the head.

Wilson felt his hobby of shooting had come in handy at last and at this point the insane notion flew through his head as to what he would tell his wife Julia when she came in from work.

Barnett was obviously dead but MacKenzie seemed only stunned so Wilson calmly and cold bloodedly, with the helpless Inspector Hyslop staring on aghast, stepped forward, took deliberate aim at MacKenzie's head and fired, killing him instantly. A post mortem later revealed that MacKenzie would have lived had it not been for this second shot.

While this was going on Constable Sellars had managed to spring into the bathroom over the prostrate Hyslop and lock himself in. He had something Wilson had not bargained for - a pocket radio. Sellars started shouting frantically but vainly for help into the radio while Wilson fired at the bathroom lock and yelled, "We'll need to get this bastard - he's got a radio!"

Wilson then shouted to Sim, who had a spare round of ammunition in his pocket, "You'll need to get me more rounds!"

But Sim only swore and said they should give themselves up.

Sellars now saw the bathroom door opening and, grabbing the handle, pitted his strength against Wilson's. The door opened an alarming inch but at this point Hyslop, lying at Wilson's feet, managed at last to make an agonised movement. The killer saw this and, relinquishing the bathroom door for the moment, decided to finish Hyslop off.

For the second time in minutes Hyslop gazed at the barrel of the pistol and thought this time he was finished: but now Constable Campbell appeared at the living room door and instinctively launched himself across the hall at Wilson. Both men fell struggling to the floor.

As they wrestled there, Wilson shouted for Sim to get more ammunition from the car but the accomplice, realising all was lost, made no move of any kind.

Campbell grabbed the barrel of the pistol, punched Wilson and pulled the gun free. He struggled to his feet and, covering the two men, edged backwards into the close where he shouted to a passerby to get help.

The street was soon flooded with squad cars and ambulances and Wilson and Sim were marched in the midst of a swarm of policemen across the road to the cells.

It says much for the restraint of the police at this time that there was never any accusation of brutality alleged against them as regards Wilson. Probably they were too stunned and, in any case, every top officer from the Chief Constable down arrived on the scene.

The drama sent shockwaves throughout the city and the Lord Provost, politicians, councillors and churchmen publicly expressed their utter horror at the deed. It was a black New Year for the Glasgow Police Force.

That evening Donaldson, when he heard the news in a bar, fled distraught to the Gleniffer Braes where he contemplated suicide but decided he did not have the courage. A haggard, hollow figure, he went back to his Paisley home to face the inevitable with resignation. The police were waiting for him and he gave himself up meekly. He simply had nowhere to go. It was the end of the road for the once respectable hard working father who had been in and out of a dozen uneconomic jobs since the birth of his tragically deformed first child, the object of his affection and despair who had been an innocent contributor to his downfall.

Constable Barnett left a 24-year-old wife and two sons. Detective Constable MacKenzie left a young widow. Both widows were understandably bitter about the repeal of the death penalty and asked for its reintroduction as, vociferously, did the Police Federation. The dead men were posthumously awarded the Queen's Medal for bravery. Inspector Hyslop, who recovered after a lengthy sojourn in hospital, and his rescuer, Constable Campbell, both also received bravery awards.

Detectives interviewed Wilson in prison about the missing McGeachie but he was telling nothing.

When the case came up at the High Court in Edinburgh two months later the three accused pleaded guilty to all the charges against them. Lord Grant sentenced Wilson to what was then Scotland's longest sentence, twenty five years minimum, and Sim, aged 22 and married with a two-year-old son, was sentenced to twelve years as was Donaldson, aged 31, and married with three young daughters. None of the accused standing erect in the dock showed any emotion as they were sentenced.

Lord Grant told Sim and Donaldson, "Those who indulge in armed robbery play for high stakes and must realise that the penalties are equally high."

Before the sentence was passed Wilson's counsel, Mr. Fairbairn, said that his client had specially asked that his profound apologies be extended to Glasgow Police for having by "his appalling actions" impugned their good name and that he also wished to express his profound apologies and deepest sympathy to the widows and their families and to Inspector Hyslop and his family.

The severity of the sentence, however, was not enough for most people. The then convener of Glasgow Corporation, Bailie James Anderson, said the punishment was "grossly inadequate and simply an invitation to murder because I honestly feel that, Heaven forbid, crimes of this nature will be repeated." He said Wilson should have been executed or at least have been given life, meaning the rest of his life, and that Sim should have been given 30 years minimum and Donaldson 25 years minimum. This was in line with popular opinion at the time.

There were petitions, questions in the House, the Police Federation had a meeting with the Secretary of State and predictably got nowhere, there were outraged letters in the Press, a flood of donations - tens of thousands of pounds - to a widows' fund, stormy scenes at Glasgow Corporation meetings over hanging and whether it should be brought back, and there were debates as to whether the police should be armed and, if so, where and when should authority be given for use of guns.

Meanwhile, Wilson was having a very rough time in prison. Normally, sentenced people who have been formerly respectable (what the villains call white collars) are sent to soft option jails but this was not on for a man who had killed two of his own. He was sent at once to Peterhead, where the 'cons' despised him as being an ex-policeman and the 'screws' loathed him for his crimes. The 'cons' sent him to Coventry, insulted him or threatened him with violence. He always had a shattered, hunted look about him. The 'screws' were arrogant and gave him more menial tasks. He was forever cleaning out cells, emptying slops, washing out toilets.

He was classed as a top security prisoner with all the close restrictions and constant surveillance which that entails. As a result of the strain, Wilson took part in the prison rooftop protest in August 1972 and shortly afterwards, along with Jimmy Boyle, was transferred to 'The Cages' in Porterfield Prison.

A month after he was sentenced on the riot charge, his wife Julia, then 33 and having been forced because of abusive letters to move to Easterhouse, divorced him on grounds of cruelty. The action was not contested and she was granted custody of the children. A visitor who was there when he had to sign the papers described him as looking like a living corpse. He was haggard and wan, had lost most of his hair and had grown a dark, straggly beard.

The bright young man who had dreams of being head of Glasgow C.I.D., then of being a big business tycoon had ended up spending the long hours in his cell working on Braille books for the blind, like Ian Brady.

The politicians, as is their wont, let the storm over the shootings calm down and disappear. If public feeling riding high could not get them to budge on the issue of capital punishment at that time then it is obvious that it will have to take a much greater and longer groundswell to get Parliament to change the law on hanging. But even if the Lords decision had somehow been delayed in the winter of 1969 it is highly debatable if the prospect of the gallows would have crossed Wilson's mind before he pulled the trigger on that fateful December afternoon.

Chapter eight:
THE SPIDER'S WEB

A personal statement by Paddy Meehan

In the early hours of Sunday July 6th, 1969, a vicious crime was committed in the holiday town of Ayr. An elderly bingo hall owner, sixty-seven-year-old Abraham Ross and his seventy-two-year-old wife Rachel were asleep in their bungalow home at 2 Blackburn Place when two masked men broke in and attacked them. Despite his years, Mr Ross put up a fierce struggle and at one stage it looked as if he would overcome his assailant.

"Get this c**t off my back, Pat," the man called out in a panic. At this stage the other intruder left off beating up Mrs. Ross to go to the assistance of his accomplice. Wielding an iron bar, he struck Mr, Ross several vicious blows on the head. When Mr. Ross ceased to struggle the two thugs then proceeded to bind the old couple with rope.

The intruders were two Glasgow villains, William 'Tank' McGuinness and Ian Waddell. Robbery was the motive for the crime. Acting on information received they had come to rob Mr. Ross of the large sum of money he was reputed to hold in his safe (some of it, it was alleged, from resetting stolen goods). Closing the bedroom curtains, they switched on the lights and proceeded to the next part of their plan - to force Mr. Ross to disclose the whereabouts of the safe and hand over its keys. To this end they beat the old man about the face and head without mercy until he told them what they wanted to know.

From the safe, which was concealed in a hall cupboard, they removed a small case containing more than £3,000. This, added to other money found around the house, brought the haul to almost £4,000. But time was on their hands. It was part of their plan to remain in the house until well after dawn, when the normal morning traffic got under way on the Glasgow road. So they spent the next couple of hours ransacking the house and drinking Mr. Ross's whisky.

After a while, McGuinness told Waddell, "You wait here. I'll go and fetch the car."

McGuinness came out of the house into early morning sunshine. To avoid suspicion the car had been parked well away from the house and McGuinness made his way towards it as if he were out for a nonchalant stroll.

But just a few minutes after leaving the house a police car drew up alongside him. The police had no real suspicions about McGuinness but wondered what he was doing in such a wealthy area so early in the morning. McGuinness, with some Ross jewellery weighing down his pockets, had a story ready for them. He told them he had been in the area on the Saturday night but had been legless drunk and, as a result, had missed the last bus back to Glasgow. Since it was the height of the holiday season when many Glaswegians made day trips to Ayr the story sounded authentic enough. The two constables in the car then obligingly gave McGuinness a lift to the bus station.

Shaking with fright, McGuinness waited until the squad car was out of sight and made once more for the direction of the parked car. Realising if he was caught the jewellery would be found, he dropped the stolen articles down a drain. Just as he straightened up he saw the same police car again in the distance. The constables also saw him but concluded that since the bus services had not started yet he must be looking for a cafe to get a cup of coffee. They left him alone and went on their way.

It was with some relief that McGuinness eventually slid into the seat of the getaway car and drove back to the Ross bungalow.

The two thugs took a roundabout way back to Glasgow just in case an alarm was raised and roadblocks were set up. They split up the loot in a lay-by and went to separate houses, Waddell to a house in Parkhead where another villain called Donald Carmichael had promised to give him an alibi for the night and McGuinness back to his home in Milton. He told his wife about the police picking him up in Ayr and said he would have to flee south to England which he proceeded to do. In his haste he had, deliberately or otherwise, forgotten to telephone the operator, as he had told Waddell he would do, to give an anonymous tip-off about an old couple tied up in Blackburn Place. The Ross couple lay bound and injured all day Sunday and throughout that long night, their cries for help going unheard.

Meanwhile, Ian Waddell was less cautious than his accomplice. He was soon drinking with cronies in a lounge on the outskirts of Glasgow and between paying for all the rounds he told of the Ayr job and laughed about McGuinness being picked up by the police.

It was not until the Ross's cleaning lady arrived on the Monday morning that the old couple were found and rushed to hospital, seriously ill. Mrs. Ross, who suffered from a respiratory illness, later died. A full scale murder hunt was now launched and Mr. Ross, partially recovered, tried to help detectives as best he could.

In Glasgow the Serious Crime Squad got wind that Waddell had been flinging money about on the Sunday night and boasting of his part in the tie-up job. They tried seeking him out for questioning Waddell in turn heard of this on the underworld grapevine and discussed his best course of action with an ex-criminal who was now the manager of a pub in the Gallowgate. He advised Waddell to call in at the office of a solicitor called Carlin and get his advice, which Waddell proceeded to do giving Mr. Carlin a wad of £200 for his trouble. He explained to the lawyer this was to be his fee in the event of he, Waddell, being charged with the Ayr murder. He wanted Carlin to organise his defence.

They both decided it would be better if they approached the police first rather than wait for the inevitable knock on the door so they made their way to a police station where Waddell was promptly interviewed by detectives as to his whereabouts at the time of the break-in. He gave his alibi and Donald Carmichael, who was also interviewed, duly supported it. Waddell was then allowed to go and he repaired to the Gallowgate pub to celebrate and, again in his cups, boast to his cronies about how he had pulled the wool over the eyes of the police.

Down in Ayr, Detective Chief Superintendent David Struthers, who was in charge of the investigation, was busy giving press conferences. He said he believed one of the men was called Pat, that they had broad Glasgow accents and that they had not left the Ross bungalow until around 6a.m. For some reason he did not mention the two constables picking up McGuinness in the area at the relevant time although a report to this effect was in his hands.

Then the Ayrshire C.I.D. received a phone call from the Special Branch who had been tapping my phone for some months previously. As a result of this so-called tip-off, Struthers and a team of detectives arrived at my flat in the Gorbals to arrest me. I was then put on a rigged identity parade (we shall come to this in due course) and was charged with the Ross murder.

At about the same time as I was being kicked on the steps leading into Ayr Sheriff Court by an enraged lynch mob, an Englishman named James Griffiths was shot dead after a chase through the streets of Glasgow (see next chapter). He was my alibi and I knew just how serious the trouble I was in when the Crown Office issued a unique, astonishing and shameful statement: "The Crown Office can confirm that with the death of James Griffiths and the arrest of Patrick Connoly Meehan the police are no longer interested in anyone else in connection with the crime against Mr. and Mrs. Ross at Ayr". So much for being innocent until proved guilty!

On the 21st October 1969 I went on trial at Edinburgh High Court, Lord Grant presiding. Two special defences were lodged on my behalf. Firstly, alibi and, secondly, impeachment against Ian Waddell and another man.

The trial began with Mr. Ross in the witness box. He told how he had picked me out at an identity parade at Glasgow Central Police Office because of my voice. He insisted the two men had Glasgow accents. Griffiths my co-accused on the indictment had a broad Lancashire accent.

He said he believed the men called each other Pat and Jim. This was correct - it was the two names Waddell and McGuinness had decided to use when talking to each other in the bungalow. I have never been called Pat in my life, always Paddy.

Then Mr. Ross was questioned about scraps of paper in the drawers of his house safe. (The Ayrshire police were claiming that scraps of paper 'found' in the pocket of a car coat belonging to the dead Griffiths were identical to paper used by Mr. Ross to line the drawers of his safe.) Mr. Ross replied he knew nothing about any paper lining the drawers of his safe.

He was absolutely certain that when the two intruders had left it had been full daylight.

The police gave evidence that, contrary to what Mr. Ross had said, there had been paper in his safe which had also been found in Griffiths' car coat. Both safe and coat had lain side by side locked away in the C.I.D. department of the Ayrshire constabulary for months.

The Prosecution placed great emphasis on the fact that Griffiths and I had been travelling in Ayrshire on the night of the break-in, a fact I freely admitted. We had been casing a motor taxation office in Stranraer and it was from there that I had phoned my wife at home thus tipping off the eavesdropping Special Branch that we had been in the area at the time.

When it came to the turn of the defence, our journey was gone into in great detail. It was established that Griffiths and I had indeed motored down to Stranraer which is 52 miles south of Ayr and that we had not left there until 2a.m. Several witnesses verified this. It was also established beyond doubt that around 3.30a.m. at a spot seven miles north of Ayr we had gone to the assistance of two girls who had claimed they were being molested by kerb crawlers. We took the girls to their respective homes in Kilmarnock and continued on to Glasgow where I arrived home around 4.30a.m. just as dawn was breaking.

When it came to the defence of impeachment against Ian Waddell, a number of witnesses from the underworld, horrified by the nature of the crime, testified to Waddell's confessions of involvement in the break-in.

When Waddell went into the witness box he denied everything, even giving the £200 to Mr. Carlin. Months later Waddell pleaded guilty in connection with a perjury charge resulting from this denial and was imprisoned for three years.

In his summing up to the jury, Lord Grant came away with the remarkable theory that Griffiths and I could have been in all these places and still have committed the crime. To drive up the twisting coast road from Stranraer to Ayr and later to have been able to have come across the two girls would have meant the break-in being like a five minute silent comedy instead of the long drawn out torture it in fact was. And, anyway, it was still pitch darkness during our travels in Ayrshire and Mr. Ross said it had been full daylight when the intruders left.

However, the jury in their wisdom, after being told by Lord Grant to disregard the impeachment defence entirely, felt there was enough evidence against me and I was found guilty and sentenced to life imprisonment.

Being completely innocent of the crime, there was no way that I would accept the life sentence without a fight. My family and a number of lawyers, all convinced of my innocence, pledged their full support in the struggle ahead.

Thanks to the untiring efforts of my eldest son Patrick startling new evidence about the way the police had handled the conduct of the identity parade came to light. It had been rigged and in a way that proved beyond doubt that the police officers concerned were involved in a conspiracy.

In the conduct of an identity parade it is the practice of the police to go out into the nearby streets and invite members of the public to return to the police station to assist by acting as stand-ins. This is what the police did following my arrest on Monday 14th July. I make this point to bring home that the men who volunteered to act as stand-ins can be considered completely neutral witnesses in what took place when the identity parade got under way.

Six witnesses, including Mr. Ross, were brought to the police station to view the line up. In the course of an identity parade it is a firm rule that witnesses who have already viewed the line up-should not come into contact with the witnesses yet to view it. To achieve this, three rooms - call them A, B and C - are needed. The witnesses are first assembled in room A, are called in to view the line up in B and are then conducted to room C. In this way, all the potential witnesses who were initially assembled in room A will end up together in room C.

When the identity parade held at the Central Police Office got under way the first witness called was Mr. Ross and the others assumed he had gone to view the line up. In fact, he had been taken to room C without seeing anyone. The other witnesses were then called and this time they did view the line up, ending up in room C where Mr. Ross was still waiting in an apprehensive state to take his turn.

He started to ask the witnesses coming in who they had picked out and among them were the two Kilmarnock girls who had correctly picked me out and now proceeded to tell Mr. Ross where I was standing in the line up and what I looked like.

When it finally came his turn, Mr. Ross let it be known that he could not pick anyone out by sight but he might be able to recognise a voice. He went along the line up until he came to where I was standing at the end, as he knew I would be. He then asked me to say what one of the intruders had said, "Shut up, shut up, we'll send an ambulance." This I did in my normal Glasgow voice and Mr. Ross said, "That's him. I don't need to hear anyone else."

Having successfully rigged the identity parade, the police now set about covering up the conspiracy. First, they falsified the identity parade schedule to show that Mr. Ross had been first to view the parade when in fact he had been last. And second, two police officers committed perjury at my trial by saying Mr. Ross had been first in and that the schedule was a true account of what took place.

When, as a result of the inquiries made by my son, the parade rigging came to light, the witnesses who were in the line up all gave statements to my solicitors. In addition, two Glasgow solicitors who were present in room B while the parade was in progress signed statements that the police version was untrue. And Mr. Ross confirmed to newspaper reporters that he had indeed been last to view the parade but had not thought anything about it.

I tried to bring a private prosecution against the police officers involved in a conspiracy against me and I told the High Court of Justiciary in Edinburgh that I believed I had been framed by the police acting under instructions from the British Secret Service.

Their Lordships turned down my right to bring a private prosecution and in their judgement said that because the crime of perjury was a crime against the public interest, the decision whether or not to prosecute must be left to the independent and impartial decision of the Lord Advocate and he had decided, without needing to give any reasons, that I did not have the right to bring a private prosecution.

Their judgement went on, "It would require to be a very special case indeed to justify a departure from this general rule, and this broad consideration of public policy must normally outweigh the private interest which an individual may seek to qualify."

In other words, in Scotland the individual has no effective remedy against a political frame-up.

This carries certain logical implications: that those who were instrumental in the frame-up were aware they would not be prosecuted if any conspiracy came to light because they would be protected by the deliberate inactivity of the highest arbiter for deciding on prosecutions in the land, the Lord Advocate.

To follow through the implications of the term 'political frame-up' it must be remembered that the office of Lord Advocate is a political appointment. He is a member of the party in power and elected by the Prime Minister of the day and is also subject to the pressures and advice of the Establishment. Therefore the law and politics are not, as the general public are led to believe, things apart. It therefore follows that a Lord Advocate could, if he thought it in the public interest (as well as his own), protect policemen guilty of conspiracy to pervert the course of justice.

When it comes to the highest court in the land the judges have simply to rely on the integrity of the Lord Advocate and through him the people advising him (including the police) in turning down private prosecutions. If the same thing had been true in America during the Nixon era he might still be President!

In Scotland, to take on the police, the legal Establishment (even more conservative than it's English counterpart) and the Secret Service and win, especially if you are a convicted criminal serving a life sentence for murder, is mission impossible.

However, there was a victory of sorts. On the 19th of May 1976 - after seven long, harrowing years in self imposed solitary confinement - I was given a Royal Pardon and released (although how I can be pardoned for something I did not do is a mystery).

This only came about because 'Tank' McGuinness was found murdered in Springfield Road in Glasgow's East End. 'Gipsy' Winning, the great escaper, was charged with the murder then released for lack of evidence. This meant that McGuinness's lawyer, the ubiquitous Joe Beltrami, could drop the rules of confidentiality and tell the Lord Advocate that his client had confessed to him in private that he and Waddell had committed the Ayr murder and that I was not involved. Waddell's confession to this effect had previously been splashed across the front page of the now defunct workers co-operative newspaper, the *Scottish Daily News* with, of course, no subsequent action whatsoever being taken. If McGuinness had not been murdered I would still be rotting away alone in self imposed solitary (the only protest I could make). So whoever did the killing did me a favour.

A few months later the Secretary of State, under pressure from M.P.s, appointed a High Court Judge, Lord Hunter, to conduct a private inquiry into the case. Immediately following this announcement, the Lord Advocate made his own announcement - any person who chose to give evidence to Lord Hunter would not be prosecuted for any offence committed in the course of the investigation into the Ross murder or in the course of my trial in Edinburgh. The police officers who had committed perjury at my trial had been given immunity from prosecution as had anyone else involved in the conspiracy. As I have said, the term 'political frame-up' implies that those instrumental in organising it act in the knowledge that, in the event of their criminal conduct coming to light, they will be protected from the consequences. And there is absolutely nothing the ordinary citizen can do about it. So much for the veneer of democracy.

With regards to the involvement of the Secret Service, when I went behind the Iron Curtain while on the run in the mid sixties I was held by the KGB for months and questioned about British criminal life and especially prisons and, especially, Wormwood Scrubs where the spy George Blake was imprisoned. The Russians eventually dumped me across Checkpoint Charlie and back into the lap of the British Secret Service who did not know what to make of the situation. I warned them repeatedly that Blake was going to be sprung, saying when and how I thought it was going to be done. I was ignored, either deliberately or otherwise, and Blake duly escaped.

When I was released from my prison sentence shortly before the Ayr murder I found my phone was tapped and I was being watched and followed. This was not paranoia but fact. It is my contention that the Secret Service tipped off the Ayr police that I was in the area on the night of the murder because there was absolutely nothing else to lead the plodding Ayrshire constabulary to my door.

I also contend that the Secret Service and the Ayrshire C.I.D. (who may have felt themselves pretty much out of their depth on this one) combined to frame me while deliberately ignoring or suppressing evidence pointing to the obvious real culprits. And when they could not get enough evidence against me they rigged an identity parade and planted bits of incriminating paper in Griffiths' car coat.

I was framed because I was an embarrassment, a liability and, in their eyes, potentially dangerous from a security point of view as well as a political one. I knew too much about the interlocking workings of the Secret Service and the KGB and suspected that Blake had been deliberately allowed to escape. Allied to this the Secret Service had no way of knowing if during my sojourn in Moscow I had not been trained as a KGB agent who would lie low for a considerable time before going into action. It was decided in certain elite quarters that I had to be put away for a long time and the only problem was the method. Then murderous events played right into their hands.

At a time when every year brings revelations of Soviet 'moles' in high places and of sophisticated wheeling and dealing and skulduggery in the secret services of all countries, the general public blandly accept fictionalised accounts in books, films and on television of elaborate espionage plots. In my case, truth really was stranger than fiction.

End of personal statement

Chapter nine:
THE ROMANTIC GUNMAN

James Griffiths was born a romantic and died a romantic. In Glasgow folklore he will go down as the man who turned the city streets into a caricature of Chicago in the twenties.

He was born in Rochdale, Lancashire, in 1935, one of a family of seven. He started to get into trouble from the age of six when he stole articles from his own home and sold them, as well as pickpocketing his school mates.

From the beginning he always had a childish impetus to be the centre of attention and this acute feeling of vanity never left him. Although taken to a child guidance clinic and put under the supervision of a woman probation officer, the stealing continued and at the ripe old age of nine his mother took him before Rochdale Juvenile Court and said he was beyond her control. The court chairman was not pleased when he was told both Mr. and Mrs. Griffiths were out at work all day and told her, "It is felt you are losing more than you are gaining by not being at home looking after the children. It is absolutely essential that you should be there to give them a proper home where they would know they were being cared for."

Nevertheless, a year later Mrs. Griffiths had her troublesome son committed to an orphanage because she could not control him. This had a traumatic effect on James who felt totally unwanted by the harsh world and decided to wage a one man war against society.

At the age of thirteen he was back in front of the juvenile Court for breaking and entering and theft. He was sent to an approved school where he became a sullen, morose individual, hardly exchanging any more words than were absolutely necessary with those around him.

After release he indulged in what was to become an obsession with him - stealing cars - and was sent to Borstal. This served to toughen him up and, on release, he joined the Army in the Ordnance Corps. He also got married and had two sons and for a time his life seemed to settle down.

But it could not last and in 1956 he broke into his brother's house, stealing goods and cash. When charged he also admitted stealing from an army camp. Sentence was suspended for twelve months and, before going on a tour of duty in Cyprus, he stole a car and changed the number plates and licence. On his return from abroad he was given six months.

At this time he had developed a muscular, good-looking, tousled hair physique. Snub nosed with wide, enticing eyes, he had a childlike charm which made women want to mother him and he had a rich line in patter. But his lies and bragging could become wearing. He claimed he was a top class paratrooper and had a string of qualifications from a public school. Already he had begun living in his own fantasy world.

When he came out of prison he found to his chagrin that his wife had been having affairs. His vanity badly bruised, he plunged headlong into a life of crime. He was given 18 months for fraud by forgery and a further 15 months for burglary.

After this he claims he managed to avoid arrest several times by making regular trips abroad, living in the best hotels and hitting the high spots, "After each job I got my money together and went abroad, living in the best hotels and I did what I wanted. When the money was getting a bit low I came back to this country, did some more and went back abroad. I've been caught two or three times, but there's more times I haven't been caught so I consider it was worth it.

"As regards violence, if there's one or two people come on the scene of the crime, and I've got no weapons at all, I'm captured unless I can do something about it. So I either carry a gun or a knife for self-preservation, and to cope with dogs or anything like that."

Griffiths kept himself fit with mountain climbing and potholing. He also loved romantic classical music and went regularly to concerts. He was especially fond of Russian music (Tchaikovsky and Rimsky-Korsakov) and had a large record collection with fixed views on certain conductors (Klemperer was tops but Toscanini was over-rated).

In 1963 he was back on one of his criminal money raising visits. Armed with a bayonet and along with an accomplice who had a gun he broke into a Blackpool boarding house. But the accomplice fell down in the dark and his gun went off, alerting the sleeping occupants. Griffiths, however, was not to be deterred. Two men appeared and he promptly stabbed one on the side of the head and in the thigh and almost sliced off the fingers of the other man. He then tried to comfort the injured men, getting a wet cloth compress. The two thieves made off with £700 but shortly after they were arrested and two guns were found in Griffiths' flat. An inspector at the time said that he was convinced if Griffiths had not been surprised by the swiftness of the police reaction he would have been ready to shoot it out.
He was sentenced to four years and ended up in Parkhurst on the Isle of Wight from where he staged a daring escape. He simply walked away from an outside working party when no-one was looking and got the local bus to Ryde where he paid for a day return on the ferry.

Although he was wearing prison overalls no-one paid any attention and he actually shared a railway compartment with a prison officer and his wife on the journey from Portsmouth to London. He was one of the few men in the prison's history to make a successful escape to the mainland.

He retreated up to Scunthorpe where he hid out in a caravan, protected by local villains. He returned to burglary and car theft but the law eventually caught up with him and he was given another four years and returned to Parkhurst.

There he met up with Paddy Meehan and Roy Fontaine, whose real name was Archibald Hall and who was nicknamed 'the Butler' in the criminal fraternity. A Glasgow-born psychopath, the Butler's racket was to enter the service of a wealthy family then rob them. He later became notorious as the Demon Butler, having murdered a string of victims and accomplices and buried their bodies throughout England and Scotland. This three made an odd trio but Griffiths admired Hall's high class ways and avidly read society magazines that the Butler ordered. Griffiths was always putting on airs and graces, talking with a posh accent and, when he was on the outside, dressing flashily with jewelled tie pins and cufflinks. He was unpopular with most of the prisoners who found him a fake and a bore. Meehan found him faintly amusing.

Griffiths was eventually transferred to Gartree Prison where he was among a group of prisoners interviewed for a television documentary. He boasted about his climbing and potholing exploits, about being a loner, about his love of classical music, about being punctilious, well-dressed, polite and well spoken.

He also was certain he would not mend his criminal ways, "I'm not going straight when I've finished because I don't feel there's any future in going straight. I'm going to get some money when I get out of here. I shall either get the money and live very well in South America for the rest of my life, or get buried.

"Under the new penal laws a man like me with more than two indictable convictions could be sent down for a long stretch, even for a quite minor offence like stealing a bottle of milk. So when I get out of here, I know I'm going to face a big sentence if I'm caught - fifteen or twenty-five years.

"Under these circumstances, my course is clear. I don't go out with the intention of committing violence. But if in the course of my going on a job, it means either I get caught and put in prison, or I whack somebody over the head and they die, that's their hard luck. And there's no point on a job in turning back because you get as much for starting as you will for finishing, so if a policeman charges at me shouting, 'Stop, stop, stop', and he caught me a blow with that truncheon, if I had a gun in my possession, I would use it. In fact I WOULD use it!"

It was almost as if he was foretelling his own doom.

On his release, due to conversations he had had with Meehan and Hall, Griffiths decided to move to Glasgow and to make the city, where he was unknown, the base of his future criminal operations. Hall was still inside but supplied Meehan's address in the Gorbals and one evening the immaculate, polite Griffiths turned up on the doorstep. He had some stolen jewellery and an antique clock which had to be reset.

He was still the old suave Griffiths, boasting of his luxury flat, his position with a jewellery company, his new expertise at karate, showing off a tattoo on his arm consisting of a snake, dagger and skull and crossbones.

Within weeks he had broken into the home of former Secretary of State Michael Noble and stolen antiques worth tens of thousands of pounds. He compulsively stole flashy, expensive cars (in the boot of one he found a thousand pounds) and when he had seven or eight secreted in garages throughout the city he would drive some of them up to Loch Awe in Argyllshire and drive them off a cliff into a steep, deep stretch of water he had discovered. This stealing of cars for Griffiths was as much for pleasure as profit. He was always driving Meehan about, getting introduced to other crooks and pleading with the safeblower to 'crack a bank' with him. From cars outside sporting hotels in the Highlands he stole a shotgun and two rifles.

It was one of their jaunts, this time to Stranraer, which had fateful consequences for both Meehan and Griffiths as has been recounted in the previous chapter. They had been casing a motor taxation office with the object of stealing documents for Griffiths' fleet of stolen cars while, unknown to them, the Ross break-in which was to lead to murder was taking place further north in Ayr.

Once Meehan was charged with murder, Griffiths was in a quandary. He wanted to clear his pal but he knew if he gave himself up he was going away for a long time. He tried phoning reporters he knew but could not get in touch with them.

He phoned Tom Goodall, the head of Glasgow C.I.D., three times and told him Meehan had nothing to do with the murder. He told him about the Stranraer situation and Goodall said he should give himself up for Meehan's sake. Griffiths said he could not give himself up.

Then the inevitable happened. Meehan had to give the police Griffiths' address to clear his name. On the day that Meehan was appearing at Ayr Sheriff Court the police came for Griffiths.

What will always remain a mystery is why Griffiths had not moved out but was waiting for them at his attic flat in Holyrood Crescent, on Glasgow's north side. With his criminal expertise it must have been obvious to him that Meehan was bound to give him away to save his own skin. Yet Griffiths made no attempt to flee, almost as if he was willing to go out with a bang. The squad car pulled up outside his flat and five officers got out into the bright sunshine. They went up to the attic landing and knocked on his door loudly, saying who they were and demanding that he open up. A radio was playing and this was switched off. There was no answer. Again the knock and again the demand to open up. Then the detectives charged the door and burst it in, only to be greeted with the sight of Griffiths charging at them with a shotgun.

Since they were unarmed and taken by surprise, the officers promptly turned about and fled down the stairs as fast as they could go. Griffiths raced onto the landing, firing after them and wounding the last man in the back. They took cover behind their car which Griffiths sprayed with bullets from the attic window.

He had once boasted to one of his Scunthorpe cronies that when he went he was going to take as many with him as he could - he was not going on his own. Popping benzedrine tablets into his mouth, he started firing at startled passers-by, both men and women, wounding several. He brought a police van carrying reinforcements to a halt and, using a rifle with a telescopic sight, fired at figures in windows as the curious came to see what was happening. Soon the air was thick with flying and ricocheting bullets. Ambulancemen tended seven injured people, running under a hail of bullets. Police dogs barked and steam hissed from damaged car radiators. Armed marksmen took up positions in houses opposite while the Army despatched a Ferret Scout car. Every policeman on the city's north side was put on alert.

Then for a long spell there was silence in the street.

Unknown to the police, Griffiths, armed with his .12 bore shotgun, .22 rifle and two bandoliers, had crept downstairs, out a back window and into a lane. He ran for several streets until he saw a blue Ford Anglia outside a pub. He blasted the driver through the passenger window then dragged him out and drove off at high speed.

News of this was flashed over the airwaves and every police car converged on the surrounding area. Taxi radios were used to try and pinpoint the fugitive's whereabouts but for ten minutes it was not known where he was.

Then Griffiths crashed the Anglia at a crossroads known as the Round Toll and staggered into the Round Toll Bar. There were six men quietly sipping their pints out of the glare of the warm noonday sun when the dishevelled figure crashed through the door. He fired two shots into the ceiling, went to the bar and said to the landlord, "Don't mess me about! I've already shot some people this morning. Nobody moves or they've had it. Give me a bottle of brandy."

The terrified landlord did as he was told and Griffiths took a swig from the neck of the bottle. One of the customers, an elderly newsvendor called Willie Hughes, nervously reached for his glass of whisky. Griffiths saw the movement out of the corner of his eye, whirled in a panic and shot the old man dead.

Griffiths then ran out and leapt into a stationary lorry. He drove off as a beat police constable commandeered a passing taxi and gave chase in the best "follow that car" tradition. Radio messages now went out pinpointing Griffiths' position as he sped northwards through the Springburn district.

In a main road the lorry screeched to a halt at a traffic jam caused by faulty lights and did a right angle up a side street called Kay Street which turned out to be a short cul-de-sac.

Diving out, Griffiths ran up the stairs of the last tenement to the top floor and shot away the lock of a flat which had been vacated only minutes previously by its tenant. Taking up a position at the window he started firing, for no sane reason, at people in a playground opposite.

The police converged on the area in force, sealing off and evacuating Kay Street. He was not going to escape this time. It was to be his last stand.

While detectives fired at the window from the playground, two officers, Chief Superintendent Callum Finlayson and Sergeant Ian Smith, crept up the side of Kay Street, hugging the wall until they came to the last close. On tip-toe they then swiftly ascended the stairs.

Finlayson lifted the flap of a letter box in the door of the gunman's eyrie and looked through. Griffiths turned at the sound of the flap, saw the eyes and made for the door, guns in each hand.

Finlayson said later, "It was either Griffiths or myself. I took my revolver and aimed it, through the letterbox, at his shoulder and fired. We then pushed open the door and sprang at him. He fired at us but missed, and slumped to his knees. We grappled with him and took the guns from him."

His feet hardly touching the stonework, the two men took the slack body down the stairs to the close mouth where it finally collapsed to the ground. He was dead which surprised Finlayson who had only managed to get off one stray shot. It turned out that the bullet had ricocheted down Griffiths' rib cage, tearing his insides apart.

That day, in just over an hour, he had killed one man and wounded thirteen others, taken on the whole of the Glasgow police force and had gone out Dillinger-style through a freak shot. He had been given the ending he desired.

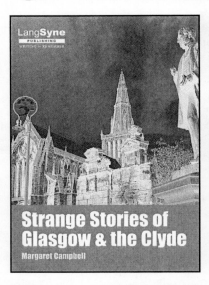
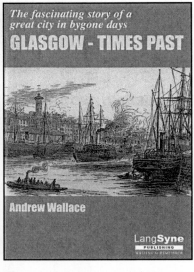

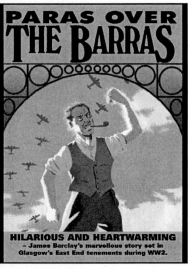